The House That Held Everything

The House That Held Everything

A Family's Hidden Hoarding and the Secrets Left Behind

Eileen Stukane

BLOOMSBURY ACADEMIC
NEW YORK • LONDON • OXFORD • NEW DELHI • SYDNEY

BLOOMSBURY ACADEMIC

Bloomsbury Publishing Inc, 1359 Broadway, New York, NY 10018, USA
Bloomsbury Publishing Plc, 50 Bedford Square, London, WC1B 3DP, UK
Bloomsbury Publishing Ireland, 29 Earlsfort Terrace, Dublin 2, D02 AY28, Ireland

BLOOMSBURY, BLOOMSBURY ACADEMIC and the Diana logo are trademarks of
Bloomsbury Publishing Plc

First published in the United States of America 2025

Copyright © Eileen Stukane, 2025

All rights reserved. No part of this publication may be: i) reproduced or transmitted in any form, electronic or mechanical, including photocopying, recording or by means of any information storage or retrieval system without prior permission in writing from the publishers; or ii) used or reproduced in any way for the training, development or operation of artificial intelligence (AI) technologies, including generative AI technologies. The rights holders expressly reserve this publication from the text and data mining exception as per Article 4(3) of the Digital Single Market Directive (EU) 2019/790.

Bloomsbury Publishing Inc does not have any control over, or responsibility for, any third-party websites referred to or in this book. All internet addresses given in this book were correct at the time of going to press. The author and publisher regret any inconvenience caused if addresses have changed or sites have ceased to exist, but can accept no responsibility for any such changes.

A catalog record for this book is available from the Library of Congress.

ISBN: HB: 978-1-5381-9927-5
ePDF: 979-8-8818-6072-1
eBook: 978-1-5381-9928-2

Typeset by Deanta Global Publishing Services, Chennai, India
Printed and bound in the United States of America

For product safety related questions contact productsafety@bloomsbury.com.

To find out more about our authors and books visit www.bloomsbury.com and sign up for our newsletters.

For my family, and for all families,
who open doors to hidden secrets.

Contents

Acknowledgments viii

Introduction 1

1 A Key Opens Locked-In Lives 7
2 Uncle Mike Keeps Time (for Himself) 33
3 Aunt Marie Reflected in Glass and Porcelain 51
4 Peter and His Paperweights 65
5 Bob's Christmas Every Day 77
6 Effie and Jacob: Family Secrets Revealed 93
7 Objects Tell Unspoken Stories 109
8 What I Did with All That Stuff 121
9 When Someone You Love Compulsively Hoards 137

Epilogue: Closing the Door and Burying Bob 159

Resources 167
Bibliography 168
Family Tree 171
About the Author 172

Acknowledgments

Ellen Stukane Black and I were partners in finding, touching, and separating all objects in *The House That Held Everything*. I could not have walked through the front door without my sister Ellen by my side. We shared this adventure together. Ellen's husband, my brother-in-law Jim Black, not only tolerated but graciously welcomed my many overnighters during travel days to Cherry Hill. My brothers, Edward Stukane and Tom Stukane, never hesitated when we needed their help to fill those dumpsters. Although they preferred speed, I thank them for understanding our slower sorting pace as we sifted through family possessions.

Ron Ford of Hoarders Express did not flinch when schedules or plans changed. He remained committed to seeing every room in the house emptied out. I am grateful for his flexibility.

I discovered the depth and breadth of hoarding disorder from the extensive studies and works of Drs. Randy O. Frost, Gail Steketee, and Michael A. Tompkins. I thank them all for taking the time to speak with me. Drs. Frost, Steketee, and Tompkins have brought unparalleled understanding to a complicated issue.

My appreciation also goes to Grant Souder, sales associate, Alderfer Auction, and John Schultz, president, National Auction Association. They personally provided me with inside information about the paths objects take to auctions.

Acknowledgments

My editor, Jacqueline Flynn, has watched over my manuscript's journey to Bloomsbury Publishing. Jacquie has given *The House That Held Everything*, a brilliant polish. I am deeply grateful to her.

Bloomsbury's Mikayla Lindsay, assistant to Jacqueline Flynn, has kept my facts on track. High praise for her precision! Another woman of precision is Jane Cavolina. She has my hearty thanks for her ability to finesse a bibliography.

Early on, when only a few chapters had been written, Dawn Raffel brought her sharp editing insights to this story. She offered me direction and the courage to keep going. Thank you, Dawn.

Finally, my family! There are not enough "Thank Yous" for my husband, David Puchkoff, who read every word and offered careful criticism. I took his advice, along with his love, to heart. My daughter, Masha, never faltered in her staunch support of my efforts.

My departed relatives gave me more of their true selves after death, through their objects, than I could have ever imagined was possible. I gained a powerful awareness of the endurance of connections and the secrets they hold. For this, and for them, I am beholden.

Introduction

"Why?" Family, friends, and new acquaintances, after hearing about the year I spent emptying out my cousin's house of hoarding, would narrow their eyes—the way one does to focus on something puzzling—look directly at me, and once more ask: "Why would you do that to yourself?" Comments about dust, dirt, mold, odors, the time taken and for what, were typical. Sometimes I felt people looking at me as if I were the one with a deep-seated issue, even though I was not the person who hoarded.

Then there were others who, as soon as they heard I was writing a book about inheriting (with my siblings) the generational home of my deceased first cousin Bob, and the fact that its three bedrooms, two baths, living room, dining room, kitchen, basement, and attic were filled to capacity with accumulated objects, instantly related, concerned that they too might have a hoarding disorder, or fearful that someone they loved was quietly hoarding. However, even these people, after they had gathered their thoughts, wondered why I did not simply toss everything into dumpsters and be done with it.

I understood everyone's perspective. My two brothers felt the same way: fill the dumpsters as fast as possible and sell the house. However, my "Why?" was about something different. Why had my cousin built a fortress of objects, from trash to treasures, around himself? Why had he become so isolated from the rest of his family after his brother and parents had died? Why did he allow his childhood home and its surrounding property, which had once been welcoming and well cared for, to fall into decrepitude? My sister Ellen shared my questions, as well as my commitment to finding answers. Together we became a team, touching and evaluating each object in the house, giving every single item time to impart its history.

I was there for the start of my cousin's life. We lived in the same building as children, his family one floor above ours in New York City. Years later, both families moved to New Jersey. Distance in miles and interests kept us apart, but like many families, we came together for major milestones. As adults, we were kindred friends with shared memories. I had no hint that Bob's life had swerved in the direction of hoarding. I was driven to sort through the rubble, the pieces of his past, to uncover the reason, or reasons, why.

What is left behind, the objects and artifacts of a person's life after he or she is gone, reveals the essence of that person. Through their possessions, I learned more about the four people who had lived in the house—my uncle, aunt, and two cousins—than I knew about them when they were alive. Their objects revealed their goals, their joys and sorrows, their fears and flaws, the loves in their lives, and the secrets they kept.

I did not anticipate the way my relatives' lives would unspool before me or that a new family history would reveal itself to me when I entered the New Jersey home where my cousin had died. Even though Bob and I had not spoken recently, our family ties, for me, were strong. As I delved into the source of Bob's hoarding, I felt even closer to him. My empathy for him grew as my understanding of hoarding disorder increased. I was somewhat shaken when I understood that hoarding disorder can have a genetic connection, and of course, we were genetically connected.

My year-long unexpected excavation plucked me from my normal routines and responsibilities and brought me, as if leading me by the hand, into an expansion of thought, an awakening to the deeper meaning an object can hold. As you follow along with me on my path of discovery, seeing how the drive to accumulate is human, although extreme for those with hoarding disorder, you may recognize familiar connections, feelings that are yours alone, for things you possess that may also possess you.

*So we beat on, boats against the current,
borne back ceaselessly into the past.*

—— F. Scott Fitzgerald, *The Great Gatsby*

1

A Key Opens Locked-In Lives

The everyday highs and lows of life are going by, you're barely noticing, when a sudden situation grabs you by the collar and pulls you out of your stated path and into a confounding circumstance, one more meaningful than you ever expected. You move through it, arrive in a new psychic space, and awaken to a deeper understanding of yourself and your family. Now you must re-evaluate what you believed was the personal platform you stood upon, the one you thought had made you who you are.

I tore through the yellow POLICE LINE tapes extended across the front door. Slowly, my sister Ellen turned the key that the officer said was "the one" that we wanted, the one we needed to set the house free. I was not prepared. Through the opened doorway, a rancidness warned us: Stay Away. I wobbled, dizzied by the smell of stagnation in the foul gray air. I repositioned the scarf I was wearing around my neck, tied it around my nose and mouth in order to breathe and keep going. A narrow, gullylike footpath appeared through the shoulder-to-head-high debris that barricaded me on both sides. My body was wider than this slim trail. The only way to move forward was to imitate the technique of a highwire walker: Angle my legs; Place one foot directly in front of the other; Slide into short, toe-first steps; Maintain balance with a steady focus. I willed myself to concentrate, but I could not prevent the escalating vertigo that began to blur my vision. I was losing balance on this path that was never supposed to exist. What had happened here?

This home of my departed relatives, a home I had visited many times in my life, when the doorway had opened into a living room with my aunt's carefully selected gold brocade sofa, antique mahogany coffee table, and Empire-style armchairs, was now unrecognizable. The original furniture, if still there, was buried under rotting trash. I knew that an upright piano also held a time-honored place within these walls, but even the piano was impossible to locate. Shock was my first reaction. Revulsion was my second. Nothing made sense to me. I realized that I was trembling and could not speak the words I was thinking: Why were they living like this? What had changed them? Over and over, my mind circled back to the same question: What had happened here? Dumbstruck—that's what I was!

My horrified eyes darted around what was once a warm, inviting home with valuable antiques and paintings to be admired. I swallowed hard and tried to understand what I saw, which was only the visible surface: accumulated heaps of aged magazines, electronics, papers, cleaning supplies, cigarette butts, cracker boxes, newly purchased Christmas decorations, old cardboard packing boxes of unknown content, plastic bags, kitchen appliances, tossed aside refuse, wall to wall, floor to near the ceiling, without a break, and high up in the center of it all, a small plastic Christmas tree with mini-lights and a tiny angel on top. The cheeriness of the little holiday tree only added to my sense of confusion.

Ellen, our two brothers (who were not with us on this day), and I had inherited every particle of the hundreds of dust-blanketed, hard-to-identify objects that, we soon learned, filled each room to its limits. It was October 2017, a month after we had discovered the death of my first cousin Bob in this, his childhood home. We were the next of kin.

I had expected to enter the house of my memory, but instead, I was in a mystery house, the house of a hoarder, whom I guess I knew but did not know. Along with the startling shock of what was before my eyes was the parallel question of whether the hoarder was my aunt, my uncle (who was my father's brother), one or both of my two first cousins, or all four family members who called this house "home."

I turned away, moved as quickly as I could to the outside front lawn where I loosened my scarf and breathed more freely. I did not want to go back in, although I knew I would have to. What kind of suffering had turned this three-bedroom, two-bath home into an unsanitary, garbage-filled dump? In 2016 my cousin Bob, at age sixty-seven, was the last of his family to live and die in this Cherry Hill, New Jersey home, a place where he had existed alone for eleven years after the death of his father. That's more than a decade of solitude, plenty of time to hide and hoard. But was he the only one in the house to tuck himself behind and beneath unwieldy stacks of "stuff?" Although I did not realize it at first, a need to understand the world I had entered when we opened that front door was welling up within me. This was personal. I was genetically connected to a person, or perhaps more than one person, who hoarded, and for me, the connection was laced with questions about my family and about myself. Considering that researchers have discovered a genetic component to hoarding—which I would soon learn more about—could I become a hoarder too? Here was a secret lifestyle. I was determined to know how it had evolved and what other secrets I might discover in this house. I needed to find the objects that would solve the mystery of who my uncle, aunt, and cousins were, and whether I was like them.

I was standing in that house in October 2017 only because a few months before, a weird happenstance had occurred. My sister Ellen, while delving into Ancestry.com to trace family roots, uncovered the fact that our cousin Bob had died almost a year earlier, on December 27, 2016. Her first reaction was to wonder why no one had informed either her, or me, or either of our two brothers who were his only kin. How did Bob, the "Bobby" of our childhood, die? At sixty-seven years old, he was the last of his nuclear family, a lost soul with no career, no spouse or long-term partner, no children or other relatives outside of us. He was the definition of "alone."

When Ellen told me about Bob's death, I immediately knew that my father, if he were alive, would take charge, advancing like a twenty-first-century Sherlock Holmes to learn what had happened to the last member of his brother's family. I could hear his voice telling me to follow his invisible footsteps. That was enough. Without any clues to lead us, we were going on a hunt to track down what had happened to Bob and what had happened to the house and its contents, among them the family photos of special memories we shared. Without knowing it, we were about to discover where ghosts hid, where secrets lay buried, and how a family home became a hoarder house.

If I had been paying attention, I would have heeded the warnings of those inner alarms that tell me something is not right, because the facts that Ellen and I faced were more than unusual; they were strange and confusing, an internet conundrum, having arisen solely from my sister's casual surfing for ancestry information. That's when she found the Legacy.com site showing that Bob had died on December 27, 2016, but had not been buried until June 2017, six months later. How strange that Bob's body was somewhere above ground for the first half of 2017. Exactly where was he? I made a call to the Gaskill-Brown Funeral Home listed in Legacy to see what I could learn. I would be swimming in a sea of revelations for the next year.

A Key Opens Locked-In Lives

I knew that Bob's mother, father, and older brother—our Aunt Marie, Uncle Mike, and cousin Peter—were deceased, but all had lived in the same family home in Cherry Hill until the end of their days. I often found it appalling that even though our two families resided in New Jersey, my father's three-years-older brother—my Uncle Mike—had resisted my father's attempts at closeness with excuses of work/travel commitments. It was almost as if closeness scared him. Connecting with his brother might have led to intimacies, to exposing truths that we would later learn he kept to himself, about his life, his parents, who were my grandparents, and others.

Mike's choice to distance himself made it harder for us—Bob and his brother Peter, Ellen, and I—to store a cache of memories about growing up as cousins, even though we were parallel cousins. Ellen and Bob were born in the same year; Peter and I, who were older, also shared same-year births. The last time I had spoken to Bob was in 2015 when my mother, his aunt, had passed away. He told me about his back pain, his inability to travel to her funeral. Although he was not in good health, I never imagined that he was nearing the last year of his life, that he would die at age sixty-seven.

"Everyone was looking for you," Matt Gaskill (of Gaskill-Brown Funeral Home) told me, "but no one could find family." This was surprising since Googling "Stukane" (my cousin's last name as well as mine) quickly brings up my three siblings and me. Any one of us (a writer, an interior designer, a lawyer, an academic) could have been found in an internet minute. My mind raced to figure out why the "everyone" Matt referred to would falsely state that Bob had no discoverable family.

According to Matt, a worried friend—Bob's friend Ted, whom I eventually met in person—had reported to the police that he could not reach Bob around the Christmas holidays in 2016. When the authorities broke into the Cherry Hill, New Jersey home they found Bob had apparently fallen off what I later learned was his favorite orange swivel chair. He lay curled on the floor just inside the front door, his life over. (The official cause of death was deemed a heart attack. We would later discover that Bob's years of reliance on opioids likely ended the beating of his heart.) Without us to claim him as kin, Bob had remained in the County Medical Examiner's (ME) freezer for six months. Eventually, the ME needed the space and asked for him to be removed.

My cousin, the wavy-haired blonde, blue-eyed boy I remembered, and the sandy-haired, bespectacled man he became, was frozen in a drawer, cryonically stiffened and again alone. When the ME sought out the Gaskill-Brown Funeral Home in June 2017, Bob was a lost soul in bureaucratic limbo, a man without a family, without any friends who would be responsible for his remains, but he was not entirely alone. He had been a brother in the "Merchantville Lodge of Free and Accepted Masons." Self-described as a "fraternal" organization, Freemasonry acted upon its long-held message of brotherhood. Thanks to the generosity of his Lodge, Bob, a Freemason like his father, received a cremation and a funeral. On June 15, 2017—four months before we visited the house—a Masonic service was held for him at Grace Episcopal Church in Merchantville, New Jersey. This was his family's house of worship, the church where his parents had donated the carillon. His ashes remained in the church's columbarium.

Bob's home had not been touched since December 27, 2016, the fateful day the police had arrived to find him no longer alive. It was nine months later, in September 2017, when Ellen made her discovery. On October 20, 2017, we drove down to The Township of Cherry Hill Police Station, with Ellen in possession of two estate administrator certificates, seals officially affixed. An officer handed us the house key, but we did not grasp its full weight. We did not understand the extent to which that key would turn us into detectives, archaeologists of the dead, excavators of objects that would lead us to the interior lives of those connected to us. I would feel the live presence of my relatives in the items they had touched and treasured, and in the process, learn more about myself.

From the police station, we drove to the house in good humor. We had yet to open the front door that would change our mood and lives over the next year. The cars were the first sign of distress, and I should have taken them as a warning for what was to come. Two rusted wrecks of once grand cars sat moldering in the driveway: a "luxury" Pontiac Bonneville was parked behind an equally pretentious Oldsmobile, both vintage 1970s gas guzzlers that would have been envied in their day, but now were nothing more than lopsided, weather-beaten, rusted steel structures, covered in fallen leaves, each with four flat tires. They were so big that the driveway, itself a cracked surface of thriving weeds, was not long enough to hold them. The tilted rear fender of the Bonneville dipped down over the sidewalk, blocking the path of pedestrians. I stepped away from Ellen's car and stood motionless, held in place by the vision of neglect. I looked up and down the street. How had the neighbors in the landscaped homes before me tolerated this run-down-looking place? Maybe they remembered that this house used to look like theirs?

The Cherry Hill neighborhood was new in the 1950s when Uncle Mike, Aunt Marie, and their sons Peter and Robert (aka Bobby, Bob, BJ) moved into the three-bedroom, two-bath, two-story home (reminiscent of the family home in the "Father Knows Best" 1950s TV series). Now all of them were gone. Peter, my smart, engaging, peer cousin, had died in 1996, a victim of the AIDS epidemic. Marie, a soulful woman addicted to cigarettes, succumbed to respiratory failure six months later. In spite of what was written on her death certificate, I will always believe that she died of a broken heart after Peter's passing. Our father's brother Mike had a heart attack and died in 2005. Bob had been the last to live in his childhood home. How father and son had lived alongside each other for the eight years between Marie's and Mike's deaths, how Bob had survived alone after the passing of his father, who had been his sole source of income, his financial support throughout his adult life, these were mysteries to me.

From age fifty-five until his death at sixty-seven, Bob lived by himself while enduring serious back pain, the aftereffects of a car crash in 2004. Not cheerful by nature, he was dour and more distant than usual after the accident, so we, his remaining family, lost touch. Our two families had been close when we both lived in the same small apartment building in what is now New York City's East Village. Our tethers started stretching after we both moved from New York City to New Jersey. For years, occasional contact was what we had, but after Peter and Marie died and then Mike became involved with a new woman in the years before he died, the "occasional" narrowed to "rare." The team of Marie and Mike, the linchpins that had helped us stay connected, was gone. Bob had never married, nor had he ever had a partner or children.

It was back in the 1990s that Ellen and I had visited this house and taken for granted the sparkling clean windows, mowed grass, and a front door held open for us by our welcoming Aunt Marie. Now I stood on browning crabgrass and studied the present scene. The suburban street had not changed much over the decades. There were the landscaped front lawns, lush green grass with no patches of dirt like those on Bob's lawn. Trimmed boxwood bushes stood guard with rhododendrons under the front windows of several of the brick homes. Decorative shutters were painted in greens, blues, reds, the front doors usually matching the colors of the shutters.

The homes on this street were cared for and they offered a sense of welcome and order—with the exception of Bob's. Laurel hedges at the base of his driveway were overgrown in so many directions, they had overtaken the four-foot lamppost displaying the house number. Juniper bushes and other evergreens under the front bay window were wildly shooting branches sideways into each other and upward over the window panes. Two tall pines leaned sorrowfully against the side of the house, and an accumulation of branches and leaves had gone beyond the capacity of the rooftop's gutters and become vinelike overhangs. And what was that shapeless drapery in the front window? I could see faded beige fabric with barely visible outlines of elephant images, fabric that resembled those thin cotton bedspreads from India that were the counterculture look of the psychedelic era. I had used them to cover every chair and bed in my own "Make Love Not War" days. This would not have been Marie's décor; it must have been Bob's. I was transfixed, heartsick, staring at a house no one looked after, no one loved. Again, the lingering question: What had happened here?

The year-old yellow police tapes stretched across the front storm door sent an added message of neglect, along with trouble. Twisted and torn, the remnants of what could be a crime or a tragedy, these official strips of plastic had withstood time and the elements. They remained as an announcement to all that something terrible had occurred. The broken-down cars, the vacant lot look of the weed-choked front yard, this yellow tape—everything in view produced a foreboding. I knew the premises had been vacant for ten months, close to a year now, but I was still pained by the degradation.

Ellen noticed that the front passenger door on the hulking Oldsmobile, the car closest to the garage, was slightly ajar. We walked over to the car and I pulled back the door. A shocking torrent of paper cascaded out from the car and onto my shoes. Ellen stepped in front of me to stem the flow. A year's worth of mail, bank statements, bills, advertisements, greeting cards, solicitations from charities, and envelopes tumbled from the front seat, over our feet, and onto the lawn. I imagined the mailman opening that car door every day during the year after Bob's death, and one by one tossing in all that paper, documents, flyers, and letters galore. As a matter of fact, that Oldsmobile was no longer a car, but rather, a large mailbox. Is it legal to deliver mail this way? Bank statements were distracting but we could not stop to open any envelopes. We had to keep moving. Since we had not yet turned on the electricity in the house, we had to make the most of daylight.

It was time to unlock the front door and fully enter the mystery. I ripped away the police tape and nervously opened the glass storm door that was protecting the wooden front door. As if we had not encountered enough mailings, more mail, finally freed, released itself from between the storm door and the front door. Envelopes and advertisements fell over my feet and down the cement front steps. Clearly, as far as the post office was concerned, mail was being delivered to an addressee at a correctly designated address. Dead or alive, it didn't matter. Once the space between the storm door and the wooden front door was filled to capacity, the mailman must have turned his gaze to the Oldsmobile as a place of postal refuge. "We had better stop at the post office to have any further mail forwarded to me," Ellen said. "You bet," I answered.

Then Ellen, with key in hand, hesitated. On the wood door, at our eye level, we faced a dusty, plastic Christmas wreath. Green plastic pine and ivy branches were decorated here and there with red plastic poinsettias, several broken at their flowered tips, and at the base of the wreath, one red velour bow, a little droopy, a little shabby, fairly dirty. Bob must have hung that wreath ten months ago. It was a leftover from a life. I reached out and touched its plastic branches, one degree of separation from my cousin now. I wished the wreath could speak to me, tell me what Bob was feeling when he attached it to his front door, whether he had reached for it in a moment of contentment or sought solace from it. The soiled sadness of what was supposed to be a happy holiday decoration had transformed the wreath into a symbol of misfortune and neglect. Ellen paused, then lifted the wreath from its hook and set it on the front seat inside the Oldsmobile mailbox for safe keeping. It held a story. It seemed important to protect.

At last, Ellen directed the key into the lock. Considering everything we had seen so far—the crumbling, once-elegant cars; the wildly overgrown vegetation; the weed-filled lawn; the sorrowful Christmas wreath—we looked at each other, and I said it out loud, "What's in store for us next?" Probably the key won't work, I thought to myself. I was wrong. With no trouble at all, the key easily turned, and the front door gave way. What reached us first was the smell, which momentarily made me lose my balance. I had been overtaken by this stench before.

In 2001, the day after the Twin Towers burned and collapsed into rubble, a north wind blew, and the odor of the tragedy reached my neighborhood, a mile north in Greenwich Village. I had inhaled the putrid air created by lives lost within burnt steel, cement, glass, plastic, wood, electrical wiring, fabric, cardboard, and paper when I made the mistake of going outside. Now, this doorway had transformed into a portal of memory as the rank odor from within wafted over me, a stomach-turning smell of death, stagnation, and, since Bob was a smoker, the strong scent of fire, of burning.

Positioning my scarf over my nose and mouth, I stood shoulder to shoulder with Ellen in the doorway as we scanned the scene and gasped at what looked like a landfill. From previous visits, we knew that the front door opened into the living room, but the identity of this room had been wiped out. I remembered being in lively conversation with Marie on her gold brocade sofa, and carefully setting my teacup on the lemon-scented wood of the polished coffee table. I think I even remarked on the table's elegantly curved legs at the time. Now, with no furniture in sight, the room filled me with sorrow, a heartache like the one I felt when walking among broken, neglected headstones in an old cemetery. It's the forsaken sadness of no one caring. The collapsing stacks of newspapers and magazines and unsteady towers of old packing boxes, the thin gray coat of ash over every surface, spoke of emotional depression, a giving up by those who lived in this house. Perhaps somewhere underneath the piles, the living room furniture of my memory existed, but I had no way of knowing, at least not yet.

I could see one familiar presence; however, the ornate carved brass pendulum clock high on a living room wall, far above the degradation below. That prominent timepiece had measured the minutes of life. It stopped forever at 10:55. I stared at the enamel clockface that I had routinely glanced at in the past. A sense of unreality swept over me like a sudden tsunami. I was in the home of my relatives, but yet this was not the home of my relatives. This disaster of a house was a world away from the people I had visited, the people connected to me. When did the changes start? And how was I so blind to them?

We crept along carefully, placing one foot slowly and precisely in front of the other in order to traverse the narrow path to the "dining" room and then the kitchen, where we found more of the same heaps of garbage, flotsam, and jetsam everywhere. I soon understood that the smoggy gray air in the house was from dust, yes, but this dust had combined with the residual smoke from thousands of Bob's cigarettes. It had seeped into the porous plaster walls and embedded an odor in every room.

I found it difficult to breathe, first from the powerful stench, then from the dust and ash we were stirring by our presence, but what really took my breath away was a fact that could not be denied. We had opened the door of a hoarder's house, by definition a place where no room can function for its originally intended purpose. It was impossible, for example, to have living in the living room or dining in the dining room. A member, or perhaps even more than one member, of our family had created this house of gloom and had existed within it. Should someone in your family be proclaimed a genius, you might wonder, in fact even hope, that there could be a link, a genius gene that you might share. Well, what happens when you see yourself genetically linked to a hoarder is the same, the possibility of a connection, but this time the possibility is laced with fear. I cringed in trepidation. All those papers and boxes unorganized in my home office, could they be the start of a horrible hoarding disease? I assumed that since Bob had lived in the house alone for eleven years, the hoarding was mostly done by him, but I couldn't be certain, at least not yet. Traumatic events in his past—the long-ago family story of how as a young man Bob was pistol-whipped by someone he had considered a friend, how his parents had to fly to California to bring him home, how they nursed his injuries, and cradled him throughout his life—these memories surfaced. Alone, without the security of his parents, could he have barricaded himself with objects, in effect created a fortress of comfort to replace his missing protectors? Or had Mike been the one to step away from sanitary routines first? I asked myself this while reeling from the sight of all the dirt and debris before me. The sudden dryness in my mouth made swallowing difficult. This house of secret suffering was making me sick. That adrenaline rush that causes the "fight or flight" reaction was flashing "flight, flee, get out while you can." I escaped to the front lawn to be able to breathe, but I would go back in again.

I had read about hoarding over the years in various articles in the *New York Times*, when tenants had reported foul smells from a neighboring apartment. These offensive odors had led to the discovery that someone had died in the garbage heap of his or her home. Of course, there was the famous story from 1947 of those nationally known hoarders, the Collyer Brothers, who lived at 2078 Fifth Avenue at West 128th Street, originally an elegant mansion house in New York City's Harlem. The brothers, Homer and Langley Collyer, were both graduates of Columbia University. Homer was a lawyer and Langley, an engineer. Their father, Herman, was a doctor, a gynecologist, and for a while, it seemed the family led a prosperous, urban life, going to the theater and the opera, but for unknown reasons, Herman decided to move out nine years after he had purchased that home. He left his wife and two sons behind in Harlem and, in 1918, took up residence on West 77th Street.

Susie, mother of Homer and Langley, died in 1929, leaving the two brothers alone in the Harlem house. Exactly when the hoarding of newspapers, auto parts, musical instruments, mannequins, bicycle parts, tools, cans, and more began—whether it started when Dr. Collyer left or when Mrs. Collyer died—is not a fact that appears in any Collyer Brothers' story. The beginning is missing, as it is missing in the story of my cousin Bob, who lived alone in his family home after the death of his father. Did the first signs of hoarding appear after Peter and Marie died and it was just Mike and Bob sharing the house? Two men alone in a family home they had lived in for decades, a home they had once shared with a wife and mother, was reminiscent of the Collyers. Looking at the rubble before me, I felt the inevitable depression that came from seeing the rot of it all, but I could not help wondering what was missing in their lives to lead them to hoarding.

Like the brothers Collyer, brothers Peter and Bob never married. Bob remained in his childhood home but Peter had his own life in Philadelphia as the organist and musical director of a church, until he contracted HIV, returned to his family in Cherry Hill, and died in 1996 from AIDS. Six months later, their mother Marie died from respiratory failure or, depending on your perspective, a broken heart from the death of her son. That left Bob and his father Mike together in the house, and now I could imagine them becoming like two Collyer Brothers, with Bob smoking cigarettes and Mike smoking pipes, and each of them immersed in, and obsessed with, different collections. For Mike, it was clocks: mantel clocks, wall clocks, pocket watches, wristwatches. I would learn that for Bob, it was model trains and tracks, and the miniature trees, buildings, signs, and signals that go along with them—plus lots and lots of Christmas ornaments. Ted, a friend of Bob's I had tracked down through Matt, the funeral director, hinted that the hoarding had started during Mike's life with Bob, but what Ellen and I saw looked like Bob's doing. In the dining room, ten years of unopened mail had produced teetering towers of envelopes dated after Mike's death in 2005. It was difficult to imagine my father's brother living in this chaotic filth when my memories were of a tidy, functioning household.

When the Collyers' mother died, the brothers were in their thirties, alone with the ghosts of their family in the Harlem house. I think of Bob alone in his childhood home, gathering the ghosts of his mother, father, and brother close to him, and never letting anything that entered the house leave. Bob had left these walls to attend Clemson University in Tennessee and then Hiram College in Ohio, but something had drawn him back. Perhaps after being assaulted when he was traveling around the country in his early thirties, he craved a safe space. Decades ago, Post-Traumatic Stress Disorder (PTSD) was neither recognized nor defined, but if today Bob's assault at age thirty-one, a life-changing car crash when he was fifty-five, and the death of his entire nuclear family were considered in a mental evaluation, I would think he'd be a prime candidate for PTSD.

I braved obstacles I had yet to identify in the living room and saw that many wall-to-wall five-feet-high piles of boxes and bags from there overflowed into the dining room. It occurred to me that this conglomeration of messy garbage mixed in with immediately recognizable items like crystal bowls, a Russian samovar, a three-tiered brass server, white Limoges candleholders, and a decades old white KitchenAid mixer on the floor that was easy to trip over—all these objects, valuable or not, had become a fortress of memories preserving the people who were once alive within the walls. Objects of the present like DVDs and VHS tapes, flashlights, batteries, and even plastic bags were also Bob's companions, but they appeared to be outnumbered by the used and cherished objects of the past.

Bob was living in pain, according to Ted, dependent on opioids to block the physical suffering that had resulted from his car accident in 2004. Ted and Bob, both the same age, had been friends since high school. Ted was open and caring during our phone conversations. He was an Uber driver, a massage therapist, a graduate of a Christian university who had counseled church youth groups. He spoke passionately about his dedication to serve others, and he was certainly dedicated to Bob. He looked in on Bob regularly, posted his mail, mostly bill payments, brought him food which they shared together, and he had attempted to help Bob plan a cleanup, if not of the indoors, at least of the grounds.

Ted explained that with the exception of driving to his doctor for opioid prescription renewals, Bob was a shut-in. From my perspective, he was also a shut-out. Whenever we had reached out to him, Bob, who was normally a little standoffish, had declined our invitations and talked of his back pain. Even sending a car service for him to come to a family event would not work, he said, since it was not just driving but being in a car that led to his suffering. I did not realize how long he had been relying on OxyContin and that along with his physical pain, loneliness had to have been his companion too. Still, he had apparently made no mention of us to caregiving friends and left no clues as to how to find us. While feeling closer than ever to him, I also was angry with him for pushing us away and in effect trying to erase us until, upon reaching a small desk at the end of the path in the dining room, I opened the top drawer.

The release of a stuffed drawer that no one had opened in Lord knows how long caused a pop-out of its contents. On top of rubber bands, paper clips, batteries, and a brass container of rings was a photo of my father walking my sister Ellen down the aisle on her wedding day. The image caused a tearful crack in the composure Ellen and I were attempting to maintain. It was not only that we were both seeing our father who had died in 1993 but after hearing from more than one source that Bob had no family, we were grateful for this proof that we belonged. We were clearly connected to this house. "I guess we were always destined to be here," I said as more jammed-in photos of us jumped out. As there was no doubt that we were branches of the same family tree, once more I felt a shivering fear that perhaps I shared in the traits of this household.

Space between the dining room table and the wall next to it was blocked by chairs against the wall holding flower pots, plastic bins, papers, and odd dishes. Large folded cardboard boxes were leaning against every leanable area. A large metal juicer was also on the floor not far from the mixer. Both had to be stepped over to get to the other end of the table to see what else was there. Finally reaching the head of the table, I discovered a checkbook at the table's edge with a couple of pens, but right behind this small writing space was a three-foot buildup of unopened mail. Flyers from neighborhood businesses and envelopes from the Grand Lodge Masons stuck out willy-nilly. Suddenly, I saw something quite familiar. I recognized my mother's handwriting and gently slid out an envelope, quietly praying an avalanche would not ensue. The postage was stamped 2014. My mother had died in 2015. I was holding this still-sealed envelope in 2017. Staring at her handwriting, her beautiful cursive that I had seen all my life on notes, cards, shopping lists, checks, and gifts, made me forget that I was in a smelly mess of a room.

I used a nearby knife, since there was cutlery poking out here and there between the mailings, and gently slit open what turned out to be a birthday card. I was sure Mom had also called Bob on his birthday, but before I mind-wandered more deeply into missing my mother, I brought myself back to the stockpile. How many years of unopened mail were we facing? How many hours should we set aside to open every envelope, or should we just toss them all out?

I imagined Bob sitting at the end of the table, writing out checks on this very narrow edge, to pay quarterly taxes or the fuel bill, and then giving them in sealed envelopes to his caregiver friend Ted to mail. He must have been living on funds left by his father because he was not employed in any sort of money-making activity, at least as far as I knew or could tell. In a way, Bob was a mad monarch presiding over a lifeless, walled-in kingdom. He could do whatever he wanted, whenever he wanted, toss unopened mail on the floor, smoke cigarettes endlessly and leave the butts in never-emptied ashtrays, and watch Japanese anime movies all day long. (I knew about the movies because there was a viewing space, sort of a trail, from that orange chair just inside the front door to a TV on the other side of the living room. Dozens of Japanese anime movies—DVDs and VHS tapes— were stacked on both sides of the TV.)

One theory of why hoarders hoard is that a trauma occurs, a divorce or the death of a loved one, and objects fill in for the loss and soothe the depression that follows. While the years of accumulation before my eyes told me that Bob must have been dealing with deep suffering—

physically he had inoperable back pain and emotionally he might have had PTSD—I felt something else, a sense of imperiousness in the environment. He watched TV from his special chair, his living room throne. He ate the takeout food that Ted delivered to him. Although the kitchen of the kingdom was unusable, he could still reach the microwave. A two-step foldout metal stool was positioned in front of the microwave oven resting on the kitchen counter. Sitting on the top step of the stool brought me eye to eye with the microwave door, which hung open. I imagined Bob sitting in this spot as he waited for a cold slice of Ted-delivered pizza to warm.

On the stove, congealed grease had spilled over the burners, traveled down the oven door, and hardened. Floor space was covered by layers of plastic and paper bags, empty egg crates, plastic takeout containers, and even a garden hose. The 1950s built-in circular breakfast nook—with its mustard-colored vinyl booth and formica-topped, metal-edged, color-matched, oval table shaped to fit—was blocked from view by countless piles of discarded plastic and paper bags, stacked pots and expired condiments, a jar of pancake syrup, mayonnaise, and ketchup. I recalled sitting there on the mustard-colored vinyl as Marie graciously served us lemonade and homemade shortbread cookies. The 1950s-designed space was now trashed beyond recognition.

I made the mistake of opening the refrigerator. Simultaneous to the putrid odor of a year's organic decay was a mass of insects that immediately swarmed out and over the edges of the open door. I slammed the door shut to trap them, but at that moment I knew that the rancid scent and the eruptive surge of millipede-black bugs would become my mental horror show, never to leave me. Dizzy and close to throwing up, I held onto the kitchen counter where I saw a loaf of sliced bread in a commercial wrapper labeled "Italian Bread." It looked fresh, as if it had just been purchased and brought home.

The thought of how laboratory manipulation of food ingredients can create the illusion of freshness in bread close to a year old was adding to the creepiness.

Yet in the kitchen window above the sink, both on its sill, and meeting rail where the top and bottom windows lock, and on two shelves fastened across the window's width, there was the beauty I remembered. Rays of sunlight sliced through the colors of cut glass pieces displayed here, and an unexpected vibrancy triumphed over the dirty grayness of the room. On one shelf, sculpted pink and red glass vases in different shapes, a flower, a top hat, a pitcher designed with three-dimensional protruding dots on its curves reflected the light and offered a hint of a rainbow as it was joined with greens and blues from other glass objects on color-coordinated shelves: the mostly pink/red lower shelf, the mixed indigo and translucent sea-blue shelf where the 3-inch opaque glass cat sat near a shimmering pale blue glass box with a glass-carved dog on its lid, and the top shelf of green, featuring a 10-inch long oval bowl formed as if a spray of green glass leaves had just blown in. These were antique pieces loved by Marie, who collected unusual examples of cut glass. They welcomed the light, enhanced it, and reflected their unexpected color spectrum into the room, transforming the garbage, bringing back the warmth, luster, and comfort of the days when everyone was here.

This was my first taste of light and loveliness breaking through a dark, ugly mess, and over and over during my time in this environment, it would happen that beauty would surface unexpectedly and challenge the grimness. I was beginning to understand how Bob might justify his ghost world because "Look at how Mom's cut glass changes the colors in the room. Isn't it beautiful!" (I imagined him saying.) Moving an object might upset the intentions of Mom or Dad, might alter the universe of their creation, and therefore, their very presence. Best to let everything stay as it always was and just add to what exists. I could feel Bob's rationale. If he repositioned any items, the world around him might collapse into nothingness, and how does one hold onto nothing? By the time this house was emptied, I would have figured out an answer to that question. I could sense in myself a growing determination to understand the motivations, the secret underpinnings of hoarding, the genetic connections.

Opening the basement door from the kitchen and descending, reaching the bottom step of a wooden staircase, Ellen and I were faced with a floor-to-ceiling wall of shelves holding assorted dust-encrusted Mason jars—large ones filled with pickled peppers, cucumbers, and stewed tomatoes; smaller ones with dried beans and seeds; tiny ones with dried herbs, thyme, rosemary, oregano. Even though pickled and dried foods can last many months, the thickened dirt on these jars meant that they had been shelved for years. I turned to see more of the area and faced another narrow path like the one upstairs in the living/dining rooms, but this time I was below ground in a roughly 600-square-foot basement. The entire space was a fortress created by boxes, old dressers, display cases, a Victrola, an old computer monitor, radios here and there, antique wooden wall clocks hanging from exposed beams, and piles of Hefty plastic bags holding unknown contents, all stacked one upon another. The only way to get around was to squeeze along that slim opening, that narrow path beside the stairway. This brought me to a raised-floor area on my left, a step up into a separate room with a washing machine, dryer, and a horizontal twenty-cubic-foot, fully functioning freezer, comparable to the size of a medium dumpster. It was filled to its lid with frozen meats purchased five or more years ago, according to the labels. Moving out of that area, I saw that dozens of men's flannel shirts, which I assumed were Bob's, had been put on hangers hooked onto utility pipes traversing through the basement's beam-exposed ceiling. The shirts in solid blue, green, and red colors formed a likely unintentional barricade.

It was impossible to know what was residing in the back of the shirt wall, as fronting it were stacks of old appliances, a TV, an answering machine, old computer hard drives, broken-down dressers, tool chests, scattered empty Tupperware containers from the days when Marie threw Tupperware parties, loose pliers, hammers, a vise here and there, more laundry, cardboard boxes filled with who knows what, rolls of foam, mountains of trash, a random accumulation of unassociated, disorganized items. The dirt and dust that coated every piled-up object as well as pipes, beams, shelves, and walls began entering my lungs and I started coughing uncontrollably. I turned without looking any further and headed past Ellen, back up the stairs, where I carefully picked up the singular path across the kitchen, dining room, living room, and out the front door. I was still coughing, but my breathing was better outside, and drinking bottled water from the car also helped. Although I felt physical relief, I was overcome with sorrow for lives so entangled in material objects. Whether the objects were sources of comfort, love, or simply friends to hold onto, I vowed to understand their meaning. Beyond the metaphysical, though, the house was a health hazard, and I had only seen the ground floor and the basement.

I went back inside and climbed up the stairs to the second floor where there were three bedrooms and two bathrooms. I wrapped my long cotton scarf over my nose and mouth, knotted it tightly behind my head, and felt very Lawrence of Arabia as the fringed edges fell down my back and I headed for unknown territory. I made a mental note to bring gloves and a facemask, and to wear only my worst clothes, jeans, and sweatshirts that could be dirtied and torn by this forlorn place.

A 1950s pale pastel green and pink tiled bathroom was at the head of the stairs. I remembered to go left for Peter's bedroom, right for

Bob's, and to take a sharp right turn for the master bedroom with an attached bath. The bathroom at the top of the stairs was a showstopper. The shower rod along the length of the tub had transformed the bathroom into a closet with more flannel shirts on hangers, but also pants and even a gray suit. The tub itself was stacked with many boxes of Christmas ornaments, new, in their original boxes—sparkly blue balls, golden shells, shimmering white snowflakes, all covered in dust. The top was off the toilet tank, and the innards were bent and broken, so this was not a working toilet (although Ellen and I soon would find one in a second bathroom). Dirty towels were on the floor, mixed with rumpled clothes that hadn't made it to hangers. Discarded cigarette cartons were underfoot too. Every time I thought it couldn't get any worse, that there could not be more garbage that could shock me, I was wrong. The categories of objects changed slightly from room to room, but it was the quantities that took my breath away. I was stuck in place, staring at the bathtub filled with boxes of Christmas ornaments piled about four feet high. I wondered whether the ornaments brought Bob reverie or joy, or whether his satisfaction simply came from filling up the empty space. I started to feel lightheaded and dizzy, and I realized that emotionally, I was coming undone.

The bedroom that we knew as Peter's lacked furniture. There was a bedframe in view but no bed, and it seemed doubtful that a desk or chair was hidden underneath the many stacked boxes of contents yet unknown, so many that I could only take two steps into the room before I hit the cardboard wall they created. This bedroom was the place where we had gathered in the dark as young adolescents. Peter had a constellation globe that could be lit from within. When he turned off the overhead lights and turned on the globe, the stars were on his ceiling. Peter as maestro, with Bob, Ellen, and me as his audience, used an illuminated arrow to point out Aries, Taurus, the Big Dipper, Orion, and more. We loved sitting in the dark and looking at the stars in his bedroom. Huddled together under that manufactured starlit ceiling of a sky, we were in our own spaceship. Inhibitions fell and secrets were shared. One summer's night many years later, Ellen and I were on a Cape Cod beach when we looked skyward and said the same words at the same time: "It's the ceiling in Peter's room."

Like his mother, father, and brother, Peter was eclectic and borderline eccentric. High above the many boxes—more stacks and stacks of Christmas ornaments—hanging in front of a window, a solid wood-like circular structure, bigger than a basketball, something that in my mind's eye was what a prehistoric animal's egg might look like, was still there from childhood. Peter's wasp's nest. He was an original. He collected and fixed antique clocks with his father. He collected paperweights. He was a musician. When we were children together, he played the accordion, but as an adult, he became a skilled organist and harpsichord player, the musical director of the Old Pine Street Church in Philadelphia. Standing in his doorway, in the room that became his last resting place before he entered the hospital and died from HIV-AIDS, I silently wept. I missed my cousin. We started out in life together, living in the same building, being preschool buddies, and I thought we would see each other grow old. His painful passing was incomprehensible at the time. I felt fortunate to reach him at his hospital bed the day before he died and tell him I loved him. Bob lived in this house and passed his brother's room every day. I supposed that filling the room to the point of blocking entry might have been a way of shutting out the psychic pain from losing a loved brother.

The most depressing part of our second-floor tour was Bob's bedroom where, at first, no bed was discernible amid VCRs, VHS tapes filed in stacked drawers throughout the room, strewn among boxes, blankets, books, bubble wrap, and old computer monitors. Hidden in the black-and-brownness of the objects in the room, and next to one of the yellowed plaster walls, was a bed, with dark brown sheets. In the bed was more bubble wrap, an empty plastic food container, a jar of peanut butter, an unopened can of tuna, and two bottles of Gatorade still half-full. It was Christmastime when this bedroom was entered last. The coroner recorded Bob's death as taking place on December 27, 2016, but that was the day he was found. He might have died on Christmas Day and this haphazard collection of edibles was most likely Bob's holiday dinner. It was heartbreaking to consider that being alone in this room with peanut butter and Gatorade might have been the way he spent his last Christmas on Earth.

Ellen and I moved along to the master bedroom, which must have stood as Bob's workroom/storeroom with its stockpile of VHS tapes and computer hard drives. There was probably a bed underneath the heaps of tapes, the cardboard boxes of contents unknown, and the ever-present packages of Christmas decorations. Also, in the same piles, something new: model trains—the kind that are often Christmas gifts for little boys—still sealed within their boxes. The accumulation of holiday items seemed a clue to Bob's psyche. I made a mental note to investigate whether hoarding could be psychologically linked to a major event or holiday. There were craft materials, glue guns, wires, beads, glitter, ribbons, and the basic glass balls that could be painted and adorned to hang upon the branches of Christmas trees. I was getting to know how he spent his days as a shut-in. He had been a painter of large canvases that were on various walls in the house, and working with his hands probably soothed his soul. There was no space to set up an easel and paint in the house, but he could conceivably balance craft materials on boxes and create holiday decorations. Envisioning Bob in this activity made me wonder how many other people who were hoarders used personal skills, devised methods, to calm anxieties and divert depressive thoughts.

For the time being, we had to leave this Unwelcome World we had entered because it was getting dusky dark outside, so we were losing light inside, and also, even with scarves around our faces, breathing was becoming difficult again. I could feel dust irritating my nose and throat and generating the coughs that would continue whenever I spent time in this house. Emotionally exhausted from everything we had discovered, we relocked the front door behind us, sat on the concrete step, and tried to figure out what to do next. I knew from the experience of deconstructing our mother's house after her passing that our brothers craved speed: fill dumpsters quickly, deep clean emptied rooms, put the house on the market fast. Ellen and I did not want to risk losing photos, family letters, or items of value that might disappear in a wholesale trashing. We could only release the ghosts of the past by moving slowly, crawling as if through a dark tunnel with boulders blocking our way, forcing us to go around, under, and over them. Anything might be buried in Bob's "treasures," we thought, and we were right. We uncovered the true stories of our grandparents, which changed family history. The greatest discovery, however, was that the hidden world of hoarding was a sign of secret emotional suffering in my family.

To take us through this unexpected turn of events, we needed help. Two women by themselves could not lift and remove a refrigerator, or a stand-alone freezer, or many of the other heavy objects we knew had to be thrown out in order to get to the heirlooms that mattered. We were about to meet up with the lucrative hoarder housecleaning industry.

2

Uncle Mike Keeps Time (for Himself)

He smoked pipes. He was the only man I knew who smoked pipes. Uncle Mike, in his seventies, is sitting at his dining room table, pressing a fragrant tobacco into the bowl of his cherry wood pipe. Close by on the table is a straight-up glass of Russian vodka. Behind him is a long maple sideboard topped with a hutch of shelves and cabinets, all crammed with dishes, stemware, vases, and dozens of objects of porcelain, china, glass. Mike is oblivious. He leans back in his chair, sprinkles tobacco into the bowl of his pipe, pats it down with his thumb, puffs inward a few times from the pipe's stem as he fires up the tobacco with the flame of a match. He closes his eyes as he draws in the flavor. He is momentarily transported. A sip of vodka holds him in the aerie of his mind. When his focus returns, his full attention is on the table and the antique gold pocket watch he has just purchased. He draws once more on his pipe before he carefully rests it in the center of his bronze Masonic ashtray, right on the "G" for Geometry that is boldly engraved into the ashtray's Freemason insignia.

Mike slowly unbuttons the cuffs of his Oxford blue shirt and rolls up the sleeves to his elbows. His eyes remain focused on the watch, and now both hands are free to open up its case and expose the inner workings that are his favorite challenge. Mike does not see me sitting across from him, on the opposite side of the dining table. I marvel at how his trimmed haircut still cannot tame the waves of thick, sand-colored hair that crown his head. Unruly strands fall above his eyebrows. Like my father, his brother, Mike will never go bald.

Clay pots with dirt but no plants fill the floor space under the table. They surround my feet. Only one plant is growing from a dirt-filled pot, and it is on the seat of the chair next to me. It is a three-foot-high snake plant. Named for its resemblance to a rising snake, the plant is a collection of erect green variegated leaves, more like stalks, with sharp edges, rather unfriendly. For me, the symbolic snake and the sweet vanilla scent of the pipe tobacco suggest the traits of the man: hidden motives paired with seductive charm. I watch Mike's crystal blue eyes peer through his magnifying loupe as he studies his precious antique timepiece. Years of irritation for his dismissive attitude toward my father begin to percolate deep inside, at first slowly, but then faster and faster, until bubbling up resentment boils over in me.

I rise, lean over the width of the table, and, using one hand to balance myself, I raise the other up to smack the magnifier out of his hand. Astonished, Mike finally sees me, but he is speechless. "How could you treat your brother so badly?" I shout at him. "He wanted your love and approval from deep within his soul and you gave him nothing. You did not even come to the hospital on his last night on Earth, even when I called and pleaded, said we needed you." My voice is quivering. I am trembling in anger. I lunge forward in an effort to strangle him with both hands, but the sword-like leaves of the snake plant have grown up, out, and around me, forming a barricade. I try to break through, pull at the leaves, but they are sharp. Still, I am fighting the stalky snake plant that holds me back and resists my pounding fists. The battle is wearing me down. I am breathing heavily when my eyelids lift and I blink. I am entangled in my bedsheet, fully awake and sweating . . . only me, no tobacco, no vodka, no Mike.

As I lie in my bed beneath the safety of my quilt, I try to understand my dream. It has been several weeks since Ellen and I unlocked that fateful front door, and soon she and I, with our brothers, will be going inside the Cherry Hill house again. I will soon be cleaning up the mess that my uncle and his family left behind because, at least in Mike's case, he, in his opinion, had more important things to do. I resent his choices. Although it is Bob who has died, I am confronting my relationships with all who have lived in that house of hovering souls. I am determined to trace the trajectory of my relatives, to find the reasons, the moments that changed them into people who collect and hoard. After all, I am genetically connected, and they became more enamored with objects than with us, or even with each other. My emotional foundation is at stake, especially as I learn that something going on in one's inherited chromosome 14 is an apparent genetic link to hoarding.

As a child, I had been able to run upstairs and play with my cousins, who lived in an apartment just one floor above ours, in a small, four-story building in New York City's East Village. Peter and I went to the same nursery school in Tompkins Square Park, played together, and built snowmen on the city fire escapes. Then time and distance separated us as each family moved to different areas of New Jersey, but the miles were never the real reason we drifted apart. My aunt and uncle shaped themselves into worlds that did not include us. As a salesman, Mike traveled, and when he was home, he showed little interest in seeing my father; in fact, he seemed to have mysterious appointments, things he said he had to do, things that kept him busy and out of sight, things that prevented brotherly visits. Whenever my father called him, I could see the hurt in his saddened eyes, an unusual look for a man who liked to laugh. I viewed Mike as inconsiderate and unfeeling. I was not suspicious until I grew older and met married men who had no trouble having affairs. Then I wondered about his actions and felt compassion for Marie, who was never without a cigarette and always looked a little forlorn and lonely.

My dream had brought me face to face with my lingering anger toward my uncle. I thought about that dream for days. I hoped the objects in the house I could link to Mike would bring me closer to understanding why he behaved as he did. Alive or dead, people exist in the objects of their lives. They remain there, in the glass and metal and wood and paper. Also, somewhere in the piles, there were family documents that would help unravel the story that we all shared, beginning with what we were told was Russian—but which we found out was Ukrainian—heritage. I was committed to the search, and the first step in this archaeological dig was to get help. It was time to choose a cleanout crew, one that would help us sort—rather than trash—the contents of the house.

The early years of the twenty-first century have seen a proliferation of junk removal and decluttering services. Since the end of the Second World War, an explosion of consumerism in American culture has indirectly created an entire removal industry. People consume, collect, clutter, and hoard, and so, we four siblings met at the house to interview two hoarder housecleaning companies that one of my brothers had selected after internet-researching many of them. Those housecleaners who came to Cherry Hill for the interview did not mention the hidden souls in the objects. Oh, they knew about them, but they did not talk about them. Instead, they were unflappable, acting as if they had been in homes crammed with boxes of boxes within boxes and maggot-filled refrigerators all the time. To them, this was nothing new. The Cherry Hill house was as commonplace as birdsong in springtime. For a cost of somewhere between $12,000 and $15,000, they could have the house cleaned out in six days. (Thankfully, the crew we finally hired was patient and flexible. Since Ellen and I took time to touch and honor everything, the cleanup took almost a year.) Fortunately, Bob left enough money in his checking account to cover that cost, and soon, opening a decade's worth of unopened mail would lead us to unclaimed funds of Mike's. Most immediately, the derelict nonworking cars, the Oldsmobile and the Pontiac, had to be removed from the driveway to make way for an enormous steel dumpster.

There was a "whatever you want to do" nod from our brothers, who would have hastened clean out of the house to a matter of weeks. Their job responsibilities prevented them from working with us, but in truth, their interest in examining the contents of the house was nowhere near ours. They were younger brothers who had not been in the company of our relatives as often as Ellen and I, and their connections with them, I realized, were not as deeply rooted as ours. Though initially perplexed by our decision to sort slowly, they came to understand and honor our committed pursuit of family history through the objects left behind.

So Ellen and I sold the cars and hired Hoarders Express (HE)—an unfortunate name for a helpful enterprise—whose people brought in what would be the first of several weathered steel thirty-cubic-yard, six-foot-high dumpsters that spanned the length and width of the driveway, a vast gray hulking emptiness just sitting there waiting, like a hungry predator.

A team of five HE CleanUppers also arrived on that first morning of work in December 2017. By day's end, we had established teamwork and filled that enormous dumpster halfway, but inside, the house looked as if nothing had happened. I realized the inevitable: we had a lot of work ahead of us. With Ron, the team leader, we walked through the rooms and talked about how we could not do a wholesale trashing, how we wanted to sort through the different collections of each family member, and how we did not want to mistakenly throw out photos, family documents, or items of personal value. We agreed to eliminate a deadline and take the job week by week. In ten days, Christmas would be upon us. We would do as much as we could before breaking for the Christmas/New Year's holidays.

I practically moved into my sister Ellen and her husband Jim's house in New Jersey. I was disconnected, away from my home in Greenwich Village. This was not my plan. My daughter was living her adult life in New York City, my husband was retired, and I was in a life situation where I could switch gears, go from the fact-based journalism of my career to writing fiction. Now the novel I was writing was on "hold" and I was sharing my daytimes with inanimate objects. At first, I was a little resentful, but then those objects reawakened the journalist in me. They held real-life stories I wanted to know. For instance, when I pressed one of the woven Palm Sunday crosses Bob had crafted for his church between my hands, I began to understand the importance faith and artistry held for him. He was a participant in a religious community, someone who wanted to show his skills to others, and not as solitary as I usually thought.

The hour-long uninterrupted drive from Ellen's house to Cherry Hill each day offered a thoughtful retreat, a safe place to share and analyze what we knew about each other and were learning about our family.

"I always liked Uncle Mike. He was my Godfather," Ellen said as she drove us past white-fenced horse farms, with browning winter grass and blanketed stallions. The dusky morning chill fit our somber dusky mood. "I sent him birthday and holiday cards and thought we had a special relationship. I don't know why he turned away from me when I grew up and went to college."

"He turned away from his own brother," I reminded her. "Dad always wanted a closer connection but Mike refused." Our communal sigh could have fogged the windshield. I continued on. "I was stunned the night I called him from the hospital and asked him to come, to be with us. 'This may be Dad's last night on this Earth', I told him. 'We need you', I told him. My God, he was only about an hour's drive away, in the same state, and he refused to see his brother still alive. He said something about not wanting to leave Marie alone. It was such a heartless, vacant response. No empathy. I think that's it, he lacked empathy. He never even contacted Mom, someone he knew for over 50 years, after Dad's funeral." I paused and then wondered aloud, "What caused him to retreat that way?" His possessions would yield his motivations to me. They shared his life. I quietly considered that Mike harbored a jealousy. His younger brother was his mother's favorite child. I was feeling, shaping, missing pieces when Ellen's voice brought me back to the road we were on.

"And now we're sorting through all the possessions that were so important to him. Us! The people he, and Bob, had no room for. They kept away from us and now we'll know them perhaps better than anyone else, better perhaps than they even knew each other." Ellen's words, flavored with a dash of irony, brought a wry smile to my face.

"What do you think we'll find in that mess?"

"I don't know," she answered, "but we're sure to discover things that we never expected. Look at how Marie left little notes in vases and glassware, and scotch-taped notes underneath plates, and chairs, and candlesticks. She left little messages to herself and wrote down what each item was and how much it was worth at the time. We have to go through everything more slowly."

"Did you notice that there was a narrow path from the chair to the TV and that the family video of Mom's 80th Birthday Party, the VHS tape, was next to the TV?," she asked.

I had been startled to see that videotape, which was seventeen years old. How often was it watched? I had sent it to Mike, received no word, and forgotten about it until now. "Yes, and it still had my note with it, where I wrote that he had nieces and nephews he had never met. I think I ended with 'Here we are, your family.'" Then I thought, maybe he never watched it, maybe the video was just another object sitting around, waiting.

"And I thought I might have been special to him," Ellen's words, barely audible, drifted off into the ether.

We try to speculate on when the hoarding began, but the voice of the GPS keeps breaking in.

"Ted, Bob's friend..." *Stay in the right lane for exit in a half mile...*

"... who remained loyal to him since high school and might have been the only person to go into the house and see Bob regularly, told me that the hoarding had already started when..." *Right turn at the exit then bear right.*

"... Mike was alive, after Marie's death. I wonder whether that's true, considering that Bob was..." *Right at the light for a quarter mile and then left.*

"... alone in that house for 11 years. How much of what we are seeing can be traced back to Mike? Also, Ted said that Mike did try to get rid of some things. When Mike tried to put a chair by the curb, Bob rushed over and stopped him, saying that Marie had one of her notes underneath the seat and the chair was valuable. At least that tells us that Mike was willing to throw something out, but then it's easier to get rid of someone else's stuff than your own." The greatest accumulation, we agreed, likely happened when Bob was living alone, after Mike died, but hoarding in one form or another, seemed to be deep inside a family dynamic that had always existed and was now challenging us, daring me to understand.

Uncle Mike Keeps Time (for Himself)

Mike, my uncle, Bob's father, was a "looker"—a handsome, fair-haired, blue-eyed six-footer. With his Russian heritage, he resembled Baryshnikov, or at least I thought so. His coloring and facial expressions always brought that other Mikhail to mind. Mike (who, in fact, had been born Mikhail) charmed with a smile and a head tilt. I guess that's why he was such a good salesman. He had worked in distribution for a major book publisher for years, eventually landing in a similar field, distribution for an academic testing company. He traveled out of town for his work, and singular trips could last as long as a week.

I had thought that Mike's and Marie's relationship, aside from their personal attractions, was cemented by a foundational heritage. They both grew up speaking Russian at home since Marie's parents were Russian immigrants, as was Mike's mother, my grandmother, who said she was Russian, since Ukraine was part of Russia when she emigrated in 1913. Throughout their lives, Mike and Marie easily conversed in Russian. They seemed to be in their own universe, where alcohol was usually present. When Marie died in 1997, however, Mike rapidly acquired a girlfriend who had no link to Mother Russia. They became one of those older couples who travel the Caribbean on cruise ships. Only Bob, who was then forty-eight years old, witnessed his father's new romance, and I was beginning to think that Mike's choices after Marie's death had likely caused Bob to experience a disconnected father/son relationship.

Marie had died barely six months after Peter, her oldest son and my peer cousin, who had passed away from AIDS-related complications. For Mike and Bob, the loss of a wife and mother, a son and brother, within such a short time, must have bathed them in grief. Eventually, it seems they each found their own sources of consolation. Mike soon entered into a new relationship, and he also had his timepieces. I could feel Mike's presence in his clocks and watches. He perfectly synchronized the seconds, minutes, and hours of life in the house. His dresser drawer held lists of the watches he was working on. Repaired family watches in wrappers noted dates of maintenance. There was a reverence for time and its passage revealed in the house, and as a writer, I liked that feeling of being in the present and the past at the same time. The revulsion I experienced when I stepped through the front door into this chaotic world was shifting into something else. "I'm becoming more sympathetic toward everyone," I told Ellen.

"I know what you mean," she said. "I think the objects are ways to keep from going under, from being deeply depressed. We're attacking stuff that Marie, Mike, Bob used to make fortresses for mental health."

Even though a conglomeration of unrelated objects obscured whatever furniture might be underneath, nothing blocked the carved brass pendulum clock that sat on a customized wall shelf high above the Everest of objects in the living room. Like a doorman or butler, it greeted all who entered. That prominent timepiece captured the gaze of all who crossed the threshold and came into the house. It certainly had captured mine. This, more than any other object, mattered, and it belonged to Mike.

Although I would find many more antique timepieces, mantel clocks, pocket watches, wall clocks, and wristwatches, all chosen by Mike and cared for by him, none would be as imperious as his elevated brass-framed pendulum clock, and carved in the high brass frame were a well-dressed colonial-era man and woman and a cart of their possessions in the foreground, leaving a background of a village in the distance. The clock's 18-inch white cloisonné enamel face, encircled by black Roman numerals, may have told the time, but more than that, it was a statement of Mike's dedication to precision. The carved brass clock face casing and the round hammered brass pendulum exactly matched each other in size. A total of nine alternating brass rods and chains, about three feet long, connected the clock face and pendulum. Cylindrical clock weights that moved time forward should have been hanging amid the rods, but instead, I found them on the floor.

Every day, the moment was always 10:55 (a.m.? p.m.?). Since nothing in the house had been touched after Bob's death, and the clock weights were on the floor, Bob must have placed them there. He had been living an eternal 10:55 existence, which would have been maddening to Mike, who always wanted all clocks ticking. As far as I was concerned, the stopped clock stood as an undisguised form of rebellion by a son toward his father. Although Mike had been the timekeeper, it seemed that it was Bob who had discovered how to stop time—intangible, precious, time.

"Do you think that when Bob looked at that stopped clock every day he ever thought about winding it up and making it work?" I asked Ellen. "I wonder whether he just wanted to separate from his father in a major way, not care about what was important to Mike or what he left behind."

"Looking around here, I don't think he cared about much at all, his things, Mike's treasures, anything," she said, and taking in the sight before me, I had to agree that that certainly seemed so.

With Mike's clocks, watches, and, to a lesser degree, stamps, and old coins, poorly cared for and turning up in every room in unexpected ways, beneath tattered boxes, in envelopes hidden in drawers, within the pages of books, I began to question whether someone who considers himself to be a collector could be fooling himself and actually be suffering from a hoarding disorder. I knew that collectors sought certain categories of items, like stamps or coins, liked to proudly display their collections, and kept them well-organized. Mike spent decades obsessing over timepieces that we found covered in dead bugs and dust on shelves upstairs in bedrooms and downstairs in the basement. Ornately carved mantel clocks and certain antique silver pocketwatches looked quite valuable (and they turned out to be so). However, I saw little evidence that he displayed them as a collector would, but did that make him a borderline hoarder?

Mike made lists. I found them with his ledgers, letters, and in the mess of the environment, I felt he had a sense of order. This organizing, to me, did not fit with someone who would allow himself to live in chaos, in rooms that no longer functioned for their stated purpose. Yet Bob's friend Ted said that accumulation had started "a little" when Mike was still alive, implying that Mike had participated in the gathering.

Ellen and I talked about what Ted had told us as we pulled open Mike's dresser drawers. His underwear was still neatly folded although he had been gone a dozen years. "If Ted is right, then perhaps Mike's sense of order collapsed after Peter and Marie died," I said. "Maybe," Ellen answered, "but Mike made clearly outlined travel plans with his new girlfriend Edna that I found in his desk." I had no way of knowing whether Ted was correct. He could have been giving me an accurate account, or he could have been trying to portray Bob more positively, in a better light, as a little less responsible for the mountainous piles of everything, the evidence of a fear of disposing of things—clinically recognized as "disposophobia"—a word I discovered when this house prompted me to research hoarding. I found the word amusing, although the condition was not.

In a way, my father was like his brother. Everything had a place, and Dad repaired things too—not watches or clocks, but the family car, bicycles, the lawn mower, our shoes—really anything broken. He also created full structures: a garage, a bedroom, an outdoor patio, and as far as keeping records, well, he was an accountant. These two men who were raised by their Russian-speaking single mother who supported them by doing piecework in New York City sewing factories—another job requiring precision—had few items to call their own in childhood, yet they were obsessed with specificity and the details of how things worked. Bob, however, had lived alone in the house for eleven years after his father's death, in whatever manner he chose, without a nod to order or organization. I once stayed on an island in Maine where there was no police department, sheriff, or any other form of authority. Old cars were left to rot in the woods. Twelve-year-old children drove pickup trucks. Household garbage was tossed off fishing boats into the sea. With no one around to set rules, there were none. In his solo years, because he could, I believe Bob decided to live without rules. Every day that I was in the house, objects were giving me a greater understanding of the people who had possessed them.

Whether the many mantel clocks in the house, which did not appear to have had much care bestowed upon them, were differently arranged during Mike's lifetime would remain one of the many unknowns. I saw mantel clocks on basement shelves and in my cousin Peter's bedroom bookcase. Plastic storage bags had been used to cover and protect clocks and faces of clocks. The bags had aged. No longer clear, they had reverted back to the oily brown of their petroleum origins. Tick... Tock... Tick.

I lifted a sticky old bag covering a carved mantel clock. My hand swept over wild bronze horses as they charged over a hill that formed the face of a clock. Behind the horses came a cowboy, lasso by his side, on his own steed, charging uphill in a chase for horses he would never corral. The clock face had separated from the frame of the clock. I held it in its separate plastic bag of protection and imagined Mike postponing the needed repair. "I'll prop the clock face and inner workings in this bag, and fix everything later," I fantasized him saying to himself. In my mind's eye, he sets the clock of blackened bronze horses on one of the basement's wooden shelves and turns his attention to the sandstone clock that holds symbols familiar to him. At the highest point of the arched frame of the sandstone, a sculpted wolf stands with his head hanging downward toward the clock face. A blanket draped over the wolf's ribcage bears the Masonic symbol, the compass and the carpenter's square, two "Vs," one upside down, one right side up, with their stems creating a central space occupied by a G, for Geometry (although the Freemason "G" has sometimes been interpreted as standing for God). Mike's timekeeping and his attachment to an organization noted for its secret signs and passwords meet in this one object.

Working on timepieces took patience, hours and hours alone, away from family. The Masons also pulled Mike away from his family. He was at home in a male organization with rituals, special garb, hats, sashes, medallions, and a local lodge leader designated as "Worshipful Master," the title given to leaders of Masonic lodges across the globe. Perhaps the Masons satisfied his need to be away from family while still staying social, like the nineteen-year-old he once was, the guy who went on a road trip from New York City to Montreal in 1937 with five other friends his age, and then wrote about it. He had separated himself from his family, his mother and brother, then too, and as it was with the Masons later on, he was safe within a friendly group of men, bonded in a mutually created world.

Found in the drawer of a secretary desk were nine single-spaced typed pages with a handwritten cover page where he referred to himself as "Mitchell," his middle name: "Arranged and Compiled by Mitchell Stukane, July 20, 1937." These pages contained the exuberance of the nineteen-year-old that he was, and the adventurer he hoped to be: "The day to which five rambling romeos [sic] have been looking forward has arrived. At exactly 7:10, a 1931 Ford stopped in front of my house. I was hastily pushed into the rear seat amid a large assortment of blankets, rope, food and various other camping necessaries."

This was a young man I was meeting for the first time, who wrote of his trip with his four friends, Al, Bill, Joe, and Vonya, as they tackled flat tires, thunderstorms, arguments with people they encountered, and nights spent sleeping on the side of the road, before they finally reached Montreal. Once there, they got "half-plastered and were feeling in the best of spirits." Mike was all fun with others, but it seemed those who loved him and wanted him close were the ones he kept at a distance. Even the few anniversary and birthday cards from him that Marie had saved in her dresser drawer were just signed "Mike," no "Love, Mike" or any other words of affection. Happy Anniversary, the card proclaimed, followed by "Mike." I was understanding the true divide between my uncle and my father. I was slowly coming to believe that Mike did not deeply relate to anyone. My father, on the other hand . . .

"You have to take care of each other. You're family. You should matter more to each other than to anyone else," Dad would say to me, my sister, and my two brothers. He was almost fanatical about family members being essential to one another. "Sure, Dad, sure," I remember my teenage self saying. I thought he was being overly emphatic, overly persistent, but I chalked it up to his background. A boy who was told his father had died when he was two years old, he grew up begging for offal from the neighborhood butcher of the Russian community that filled the tenements on what was once considered part of the lower East Side, but is now the East Village. His mother, Effie, of the steel spine and determined nature, cherished her two sons, Mikhail and Anatoly, who would later change their names to Michael and Edward. I understood the difficulties of my father's childhood, but I still found it odd that he never visited his father's grave in a cemetery, nor did he possess photos of his father. My grandfather seemed more ghostlike than dead. Mike knew his father for the first five years of his life but he never spoke of him. Of course, the house would later reveal the truth about that relationship.

My pipe-smoking, cocktail-drinking, jokey, self-centered uncle could immerse himself in antique timepieces, vintage stamps collected in fat albums, and coins in containers. These objects spoke of a solitary being, using artifacts of the past to escape the ordinariness of the present, but gregarious was the way he presented himself, the guy up for the next adventure. I was understanding the complexity of the man, and the question that nagged: Are they always disparate—the face each of us presents to the world and the face that our saved objects reveal? When I wasn't working in the Cherry Hill house, I started looking at my own objects at home and wondering what they said about me to others. I had stuffed bookshelves with books stacked sideways on top of vertically placed books, too many being saved for reasons long forgotten. I rarely referred back to books I had read, and only re-read a few chosen ones from time to time. Yet I could not let them go. They were part of who I felt I was. I also knew that in the hidden nooks of these shelves were the contained ashes of my three beloved departed cats. I could not let them go either. Like someone who hoards objects for the comfort they offer, I found comfort—the comfort of remembrance—in having those ashes nearby.

On the practical side, days in Cherry Hill were filled with so many what-may-be-valuable discovered items that Ellen had to rent a storage unit about two miles away to provide a place to sort. We were often in the dark about the worldly worth of the objects we were pulling out of debris, releasing from their material tombs, although we did know when a Robert Rauschenberg signed and numbered lithograph entitled "Winner" appeared in the attic that we ought to call an art auction house. Soon we were at the end of December 2017. The Christmas/New Year's holidays were closing in. Although we had filled three 30-cubic-yard dumpsters, the house still looked full of stuff. We had prepared for a holiday break by installing an ADT security system shortly after we had the electricity restored.

Before the discovery of Bob's death, Ellen and I had spent a year's time, from mid-2015 to mid-2016, sorting through and cleaning out the two-bedroom home our mother had lived in for thirty years. Now we were sharing another stretch of togetherness. As children four years apart, we had our own friends and separate interests. I was four years older, but I was five grades ahead of my sister, and while I was the oldest at home, I was always the youngest, and usually the tallest, in my class. Growing up, my own friends and issues—like being taller than all the boys—took my attention. Our life patterns resembled two waves traveling on different frequencies, sometimes higher or lower, moving faster or slower, until finally, thankfully, settling at the same velocity in present day.

What mutually scared us now was learning that hoarding often runs in families. At least three research studies had connected genetic markers, a unique pattern on chromosome 14, to hoarding. The question most important to me was: Who might have had the unique chromosome 14 first, Uncle Mike, who was my blood relative, or Aunt Marie, whose relation to me was by her marriage to Mike? I had an office cluttered with boxes of old research and photos, and bookshelves overly stuffed, but I was not a collector of eclectic objects, and I was not a hoarder who filled a room with flotsam and jetsam and made it unusable. Still, I kept wondering how many degrees of separation existed between this situation and me. If life became stressful for me, or solitary, would epigenetics play its hand and lead me to a hoarding disorder? Would my future ever hold a pattern like Bob's?

3

Aunt Marie Reflected in Glass and Porcelain

"Look at the wall until I tell you to turn around," Aunt Marie instructed us in her gravelly voice that belied too many cigarettes. Ellen and I were sitting at the foot of our aunt's bed in the master bedroom. We shared puzzled looks but did as instructed. Although it felt rude and wrong, we turned our backs to her, gave each other the side-eye, and studied the gold-gilded Russian icon of a haloed Jesus Christ, hand raised in a blessing above her bed's headboard.

Ellen and I had not visited Marie in Cherry Hill in a long time, so we made a date to see her and catch up. It was about 1990. She was around seventy-five years old and suffering from arthritis in her joints and neuropathy in her feet. Walking and moving had become painful. We brought pastries and brewed tea, and the three of us sat at her dining room table. Afterward, she said she wanted to show us some of the jewelry she had collected over the years, upstairs in her bedroom. She climbed the stairs slowly but with assurance in her motion. She seemed energized at the prospect of showing off what had become a collection of mostly vintage costume and designer jewelry sets from her younger years of dressing up to clerk in a Manhattan office. "I always coordinated colors. My jewelry complimented my clothes perfectly," she said, speaking to our turned backs, explaining how stylish she felt when she walked along New York City streets during those days from the mid-1930s to the mid-1940s. Like a young Ginger Rogers in the old classic movie *Kitty Foyle*, I thought.

"OK, you can turn around now," Marie announced as she stepped from behind a bedroom chair blocking what appeared to be a small apothecary cabinet. Did she think we would become overly curious if we glimpsed more than she wanted to reveal, or was she just being secretive to see the surprise in our eyes? She had no daughters, no daughters-in-law, no other nieces. Ellen and I would have been delighted to hear the stories of where she was, who she was with, and when she wore a certain strand of pearls, for instance. It was not the objects themselves but the pieces of her life that fascinated us. Still, she stayed with the jewelry. "Here see this, Schiaparelli," she said, showing us the stamped name on the back of a necklace of sizable semi-precious stones. "See, this is worth something," she said as she turned away, put the Schiaparelli pieces on her dresser, and picked up something else. "Here, you can have these instead," she said, handing each of us non-Schiaparelli, but still beautiful, long glass-beaded necklaces, one mostly red and black, the other mostly celadon-colored.

"Thank you, Aunt Marie. These are lovely," I said, but she was already turning away and doing something to hide her Schiaparelli pieces before she faced us again. Ellen and I shared an equal amount of eye-rolling when she wasn't watching. We knew that she harbored a level of paranoia, one that she herself had revealed on a prior family visit. Explaining to our mother that she did "not want people to know what I have," Marie described how she had taped brown paper inside the mullioned glass of the dining room's French hutch doors. That way, no one could see the four shelves of her crowded-together antique objects, jade carvings, and porcelain Asian artifacts, but then, neither could Marie herself view and admire her own collections. At the time, we did not think that her reference to "people" applied to us since we were family. Now her lack of trust, her need for caution around us, saddened our long relationship. We were among the "people" she wanted to keep away from her treasures.

Both Mike and Marie were coming into sharper focus. Mike's possessions spoke of a world exclusive to himself, a world apart from his wife and sons. With nowhere else to go, Marie created a private island, an oasis of beautiful objects. When I found her attic boxes—over one hundred that had not been opened in decades—I realized that she rarely exposed her many carefully collected pieces of glass and porcelain, vases, teapots, sculpted miniatures, to daylight. Only she knew what she owned, and only she could partake of their beauty, but unless she climbed the attic stairs and squatted down in the low-ceilinged space, she hardly enjoyed the company of her packed-away collections. The amassing of items was her secret, not the buying and selling, not the touching and viewing of them. Yet she did not ignore them entirely. She took time to write notes about the origins and values of certain favored, special objects.

Ubiquitous tiny scraps of paper in her handwriting were scotch-taped onto or folded into each precious item. For example, a Victorian high-heeled, high-button, 5-inch white porcelain shoe was noted as 1900 Russian, and although she probably picked it up for a dollar, she wrote that it was valued at $25 when she researched Antique Trader magazine in 1990. Her self-satisfaction became my own as I peeled away or unfolded notes that described how her purchases had increased in value. As I learned from a representative of a high-end auction house, collectors buy and sell, while hoarders never let anything go. Marie was saving and organizing like a collector, and she may have been buying, but I saw no evidence of selling. She clearly loved her things and held onto them, but they did not turn the rooms in the Cherry Hill house into unlivable areas. The house continued to function normally. Marie seemed to me in a category all her own: a non-selling collector—but not a hoarder.

Since Ellen and I had visited the house when rooms were as they are traditionally expected to be, with chairs, unobstructed tabletops holding only a glass or two, a sofa that a person could sit on, I could now imagine Marie at her dining room table poring over the antique magazines that she must have subscribed to, and trying to find objects that were similar to the ones she owned. Take the elaborately crafted Chinese porcelain wine pot in the hutch that I could now open freely. The pot was a pitcher about six inches wide, but quite narrow, barely two inches. It stood ten inches tall and curvy, swirled in shape like a musical G-clef. Pale green served as a background color to black-line-painted flowers surrounding the main subject, a line painting of a robed, bearded Chinese holy man, staff in one hand while the other hand was outstretched holding some sort of fruit. An ominous vulture-type bird flew over the man's head as he dared it with a stare. This was on one side of the pot. On the other side was a drawing of a different kind of robed, bearded Chinese man, one brandishing a sword. A 1976 letter to Marie from an antique trader was folded behind the pot. It stated: "Your wine pot appears to be dated from the Kuang Hsu period c. 1875 to 1908. Value, if in perfect condition, would be several hundred dollars." This surely would have given Marie a shot of self-esteem, but the wine pot never left its home on the hutch shelf. It was there for me to reach in and hold, which I did.

In my hands, Marie's Chinese wine pot whispered its Asian history to me. I could also sense that for Marie, this pretty piece of pottery was a tether to a larger, exotic world. I felt lifted out of myself. I was with Marie, outlining the Chinese robe with my fingertip and smiling. This connection must be what collectors feel, and hoarders experience: a sense of touching where a touch has come before, an awareness of an aliveness that still exists. Marie left me insights into what she might have been discovering about herself and her possessions when she wrote in classically beautiful cursive on journal pages entitled "*Reasons for Collecting*":

> *Most people need enthusiasm or desire to learn*
> *Mental Tonic*
> *Therapeutic*
> *Artistic – Accustom our minds to beauty*
> *Individuality – For home or self*
> *Historical*
> *Monetary – There is always at least 70% return on antiques when sold.*
>
> And as an addendum, this note: *Try to teach your children early to appreciate quality etc.—Keeps them out of trouble.*

She had offered her own self-analysis. She was a woman of the post-World War II generation who wanted something to hold onto beyond the prescribed wife-and-mother roles. She examined her motives, tried to understand her need to "collect," and delved into her psyche for her "reasons." Marie was ahead of her time.

(On a historical note, I learned that the word "collect" was coined in the 1600s when it referred to literary anthologizing, but the word evolved when "collecting" became an elite activity, a status symbol, in the 1700s and 1800s. Wealthy aristocrats created special cabinets—like Marie's hutch—for their collections of art, books, fossils, and shells, collections that often led to the creation of museums.)

I wanted to know what drove Mike, who was devoted to his watches and clocks, and Marie, who was so proud of her Asian porcelains and cut glass pieces, to prefer to spend more time with their collections rather than with each other. They seemed to share a common interest in creating collections, and having common interests is often a good means of bringing two people closer together. Mike's and Marie's collections were not the same, however, and judging by the accumulation of items in different categories, stored in different parts of the house, it appeared that their interests diverged quite a bit, but what if they didn't? I handed the wine pot to Ellen and found myself rambling, "What if Mike and Marie sat at this dining room table and together compared the value of a pocketwatch or a sculpted piece of jade? Maybe it's just wishful thinking but I would like to picture them discussing and enjoying their his-and-her objects, laughing together."

"And smoking," said Ellen, "Marie on her Lucky Strikes, Mike on his pipe."

I could not shake the possibility, however, that instead, they probably each retreated into their collections without sharing their common ground. I could see how, in choosing, arranging, and classifying their collections, each of them was creating a private world, a kind of sanctuary against inner demons, an environment no one else was invited to join.

One day in a New York City thrift store, I stumbled upon the 2019 book *Inside the Head of a Collector* by Shirley M. Mueller MD, a neurologist and a collector of Chinese porcelain. I was fascinated by how Dr. Mueller's contemporary reasons, what she called "pleasure reinforcers" for collecting, remarkably mirrored Marie's: "pride in acquiring exquisite objects . . . possession for comparatively little money . . . a sense of history . . . intellectual satisfaction . . . friendships forged . . . the enjoyment of arranging and rearranging a collection . . . the anticipation of the reward." As I held the book in my hands, I thought how terrific it would have been if Marie and Shirley had met.

In her hutch and on her sideboard, Marie's neat groupings of items were not chaotic accumulations of hoarded "stuff." Although Marie may have been depressed by the emotional absence of Mike and disappointed over her two sons never marrying—her discomfort over

Peter's homosexuality was palpable—as proven by our family visits and photos, her home was uncluttered and warm. I wished she were still alive so I could acknowledge to her how I understood that she was finding her purpose, filling an emotional void, by creating collections.

Born in the same generation as Betty Friedan, Marie figured out how to get out of the house and earn money on her own long before *The Feminine Mystique* was published. In the 1950s, Marie was a "Tupperware Lady" who would arrange for neighborhood women to hold Tupperware parties, or she would create a Tupperware party herself, in her own home, to sell what are now considered to be historic plastic containers. She loved the gathering together, the sales, the income. The money gave her a sense of independence and pride. Whenever our two families visited together, Marie, with great aplomb, would bestow upon us the latest Tupperware product. Not only did we have the original pastel-colored sets of plastic bowls with clear plastic tops, but there were also the specialty items: the "Pie Taker," the "Dip 'N Serve Serving Tray," the round "Cake Taker" with a handle. She gave us lessons in how to "burp" the covers, which meant putting pressure on the center of the cover and lifting an outer edge of the lid just a little, not too much, but just enough to let some air out. "The release of air ensures food freshness within the container," explained Marie as if she were making a sales pitch to a dozen homemakers. The Tupperware "Head of Lettuce Keeper," a pale green plastic bowl that came with a removable spike insert at its base, was a presence in my mother's refrigerator until the day she died in 2015.

I discovered dozens of Tupperware products in the basement of the Cherry Hill house, some with cracked covers, some with cracked bowls, some good as new. Plastic can dry out and break apart over the course of decades, but not always. Every tiny container, larger bowl, specialty item like a salt shaker, a companion pepper shaker, a pitcher, and a covered serving tray spoke of one woman taking a stand for her worth in a culture that placed women strictly in the kitchen. How ironic that what Marie was using to take herself out of her kitchen were implements for the kitchen. The Tupperware turned up inside ripped cardboard boxes, or underneath them, on top of a carton of seashells, behind a china cabinet. These were the relics. Tupperware parties had their moment but were considered passe, sometimes even laughable, when feminism emerged as a cultural force in the 1970s. Women were encouraged to become more equal in the workplace. I was on the front lines, one of those marchers for Equality. The cutting board was being exchanged for the boardroom. I picked up a pale pink plastic Tupperware bowl from the basement floor where it rested against a box of marbles. As I held and turned the bowl, I understood how lost Marie must have felt when the culture moved women out of the home and into the office. In her fifties at that point, she was not going out to look for a job. "Collecting" offered solace and provided a way for her to hold onto her self-esteem.

In January 2018, shortly after New Year's and three months after our first visit, Ellen and I decided to spend a day in Cherry Hill without the CleanUppers. Objects were still piled waist-high. Three 30-cubic-yard dumpsters had already been carted away, but we had little sense of accomplishment. "Why is it still so full of stuff in here?" I said more loudly than I should have. The living and dining rooms remained packed, and in addition, something else was wrong. On the dining room floor, the upside-down glass jug from an old office water cooler held an icy sheen. Removing my gloves, my hands became cold. The house was almost as frigid inside as outside, where the temperature was barely 20 degrees.

As I moved forward through the dining room, a crunching came from under my feet. Ice had formed on the floor. A stream of water from the kitchen faucet was frozen in place over a solidly iced sink.

Two pots in the sink could still be seen through the transparency of the ice, which, when it was running water, had overflowed, spilled onto the floor, and transformed the kitchen into an ice floe.

"I think the house is trying to make us leave," said Ellen.

This was a strange turn of events. I shifted my focus to think.

In the window over the iced-in kitchen sink, Marie's shelves of color-arranged cut glass vases, cleverly sculpted so that a pink blossoming flower, a blue tree trunk with a spigot as if sap were to flow from within, and an amber upright corncob, each on different shelves, presided over the madness with beauty. Marie's "Reasons for Collecting" with her "Artistic-Accustom Our Minds To Beauty" category momentarily flashed across my mind. In this crisis, above the sink that was now a frozen pond, a kitchen sink where she stood every day, she had created a colorful artistry that I could still see and touch. Marie, whose collector notes show that she sought to connect with history and beauty, had at that moment connected with me too.

Ellen and I carefully worked our way across the frozen floor to the basement staircase. We knew we had to check on the boiler and also knew that it was surrounded by boxes and electronic equipment, monitors, DVD, and CD players.

"Thank God we got some things out of this basement last month," I said while starting to move items in front of the boiler.

"Watch it," Ellen shouted as I accidentally dropped a box of extension cords on her foot.

We were both chilled and frustrated. Finally, I could touch the boiler, the cold, non-functioning boiler. We headed back to Ellen's house to call repair people. This was an unexpected setback. Now my hoarder house experience would last even longer.

An apparent draft had snuffed out the furnace's pilot light and the pipes had frozen, the heating technician reported to us after he had a chance to look over the situation. "What we have here is called a reverse draft," our overalled, ski-jacketed, wool-capped repairman told us. A CleanUpper had inadvertently turned on the attic fan during one of our forays up there. "The fan is sucking the air out of the house, pulling it up, creating a reverse draft that put out the pilot." He led the way to the fan switch that was mounted next to the top of the ladder-like steps to the attic, and flipped that switch to "Off." Spinning Stopped... Problem Solved... sort of...

The pilot light would keep its flame and we would have glorious warmth, but turning up the heat would transform the kitchen glacier into a watery mess. Also, ice frozen inside plumbing pipes would melt, becoming water within ice-cracked pipes, water that would pour through the walls. I was no longer deconstructing a family home. Instead, I was trying to keep it from falling down around us. Ellen and I placed flattened U-Haul cardboard boxes on the floors of the kitchen and bathroom to absorb the meltdown that was going to happen. The CleanUppers would arrive in the morning to bale and mop. Soon enough we would see leaks break through the walls.

We were ready to leave the house for the night. The table next to the front door held an assortment of objects unrelated to each other. Before we left for the day, I reached across them—the large envelope marked X-ray, Bob's flip phone, a takeout pizza menu, a spray can of paint, keys, headphones, and plastic bags—to sync the table lamp to its timer. I knew this lamp. It was a favorite of Marie's. The dark red soapstone carving that formed its base had seared itself into my mind's eye when I was five. I never saw the carving, the monkeys in the carving, as static. The carving, the monkeys, were always alive to me, any minute they might leap into the air.

I liked wearing the homemade crepe paper hat Aunt Marie had placed on my head at my cousin Peter's fifth birthday party. I was already the older cousin since I had turned five a few months earlier, and so I felt wiser, more grown-up. I definitely had the edge over my sister Ellen and cousin Bobby, who were both only a year old and barely walking. Pretty soon the cake would be coming, and I was practicing patience, sitting on the sofa next to an end table where the reddish-brown stone lamp, one I knew well, was awfully close to me. I believed the monkeys on the lamp moved, but not while I was watching them. This was no ordinary lamp base. Monkeys were crawling up the sides of two jugs; one was shorter and smoother, and the other jug was taller, with something that looked like stony ooze dripping down around the outside. To me, it seemed that the monkeylike creatures, because I was uncertain whether they were actually monkeys, on the taller jug were in a battle to overcome the overflow. The animals were crawling upward, ascending, while the ooze was descending. It appeared the monkeys were making progress and had almost reached the rim of the jug. Some days they were defeated and entangled. I did not want to be close to this collision of worlds, the war happening between animal and element every day, whether the lamp was giving light or not. I yearned to move away from it, but I had been told to wait until the birthday cake was brought to the table. Could I touch the lamp, change the course of the battle? I gathered my courage and reached out to the frightening scene, but as two of my fingertips rested with a slight tremble on the uppermost monkey, I was called to the table. It was time to watch Peter blow out the candles. I remember being relieved.

The Monkey Lamp was still mesmerizing, but the monkeys no longer frightened me as they once had. Although I now understood the lamp to be a Chinese soapstone carving, I had to be wary of it, to watch where the monkeys moved. This was an object that every person who had lived in the Cherry Hill house had touched every day, as it was next to the front door entrance, the first means of lighting the living room as they came and went. Over the years, surely the battle between animal and elements had been won by one side or the other. I refused to believe it had never changed, that it had stayed at a soapstone stalemate from the first day I saw it until now.

As I reached for the switch, I thought that perhaps the lamp might have been the beginning of Marie's interest in Asian artifacts. She had positioned this dark object of conflict center stage in family life through the decades. Perhaps it spoke of her own conflicts, of her own fight to overcome obstacles as she strove toward personal goals. Do each of us, without awareness, choose to possess objects that reflect our inner lives? Perhaps I was thinking too much. I did not remember Marie talking about collecting until that time, many years ago, when she spoke about her treasures in the hutch.

The house had been left alone, unattended for a year before we arrived, before we even knew that our cousin Bob had died in that orange chair two feet from the front door, but nothing disastrous had happened to the premises. No break-ins. No robberies. No structural collapses. No frozen pipes. Now, when I was getting closer to understanding the inner lives of Uncle Mike, Aunt Marie, cousins Peter and Bob, and how each of them affected me, the house started breaking apart. It was not out of the question to feel that their spirits were preventing me from going further, closing in on their truths.

Ellen and I told our brothers about the shut-down furnace, the flooding water turned to ice, the burst pipes, the repairs, but they had stepped away from the day-to-day decisions. In their good-natured ways, they conveyed their hope that we move faster, but now the house was creating its own delaying tactics. Whatever might slow us down or speed us up, however, soon became irrelevant to me. The objects in the house held mysteries to be solved. "Hoarding Disorder"—what I learned was the psychological term for what I was facing—needed greater understanding. There would be no deadlines.

We had already boxed up volumes of unopened mail that we had brought to Ellen's house to examine. Many of the envelopes had the return addresses of financial institutions and outdated dividend checks inside. I had started researching the state's unclaimed funds and discovering large sums of money in financial investments where Mike had accounts. After Mike's death, Bob had never transferred these accounts to his name. More of these bank-like envelopes were still on the floor.

Bob's life was taking shape in my mind. A decade of unopened mail became more understandable when I thought of Bob as someone who had surrendered all responsibility, who was only living day to day, maybe even hour by hour. At different times in my life, when losing a job, or when someone I loved had died, I had felt a despairing "What's the use?" emotion overtake me. Then, who cares about opening the mail or even getting out of bed? That feeling never lingered permanently, but looking around this house, I could see what happens when it does.

I imagined Marie sitting here in the dining room, smoking a cigarette and gazing at the sideboard. Not one inch of space existed between her collected pitchers, vases, and bowls, blue willow plates, porcelain cups and saucers, objects that once dazzled but were now encrusted in asthma-inducing soot from years of accumulated dust and the ashes of cigarettes. The room looked as if a chimney fireplace had suddenly downdrafted, although there was no fireplace in this house. These were her treasured possessions, collected, according to her words, to "accustom (her) mind to beauty," to be "artistic" and offer a "mental tonic." The pieces of glass and porcelain must have held her affection, somehow returning her love through their very existence. How could one be lonely with so much to hold onto? She must have felt an emptiness. Her Russian-born parents were long-deceased and her sister Olga, her only sibling, lived with her husband hundreds of miles away in upstate New York. Sister visits were rare. Marie never shared, never sold, her collections. They received her attention and care, and likely kept her focused and functioning. Her children were grown, but she could mother these collections. The house's last resident, her son Bob, my cousin, brought about their dissolution, as objects once cradled with love became coated in sticky dust and covered in a clamor of cobwebs. Now what I felt in the room was the sadness that lingers long after hope takes its leave. I did not see Marie in the sadness. Always striving, she remained in the glint of the gold rim that sparkled on her Austrian platter.

4

Peter and His Paperweights

What was "Peter's?" Three cardboard boxes, flat in design, about two inches deep, something like pizza boxes, had that word—"Peter's"—on the top, printed in letters that looked like they came from a black Sharpie pen. Emptying Peter's bedroom closet, I had removed a gathering of musical instruments, a guitar with no strings, a large plastic bag of castanets, two cracked violins in cases, a pile of African music-making gourds, each covered with woven nets of different shells and beads, and on the floor beneath the gourds, these three marked boxes.

    I arranged a wide stack of packaged craft materials, paints, brushes, glues, and glitter to create a stable base where "Peter's" boxes could rest. Each one weighed at least ten pounds. Slowly, I lifted the first lid. As had happened before in this house, amid the dust and dinginess, exceptional beauty struck. I never grew accustomed to the stark contrast of our dirty gray, foul-smelling surroundings, and the moments of light and loveliness that broke through the morass. The sudden appearance of elegant artistry was always a jolt, a surprise. Beneath the opened lid, I saw glinted reflections from brilliantly colored, glass-blown art. In this box, twenty unique, glass worlds were within twenty paperweights nestled into twenty individually divided cardboard sections, special squares of protection.

Each paperweight fit in the palm of my hand, and each sphere was an artist's vision. I cradled a glass oval about four inches high, larger than a jumbo-size egg, and marveled at what it held within. I would eventually learn that everything seen inside a glass paperweight is also made from glass, by an artist who heats, and then stretches, shapes, and sculpts colored glass rods. Inside the oval paperweight I was holding, vertical rows of delicately swirling pink ribbon alternated with rows of white-bordered blue flowers shaped like miniature daisies, if daisies were blue. These ribbons and flowers had been shaped from colored glass rods, and tiny specks of glitter-like sparkle on the ribbons were actually the smallest of glass bubbles, each barely one-eighth of an inch. This was only the first paperweight I held, and I realized that if twenty of these masterworks were in each box, we had sixty unusual paperweights before us.

Although the boxes were marked "Peter's," his involvement in building this trove, which had to have been created from finds in flea markets, bids at auctions, or purchases directly from the artists, led me to imagine that perhaps he and Marie—son and mother—had hunted for beautiful paperweights together. The artistry of glass was one of Marie's interests, after all, and Peter was eclectic, drawn to different areas of science and art. I lifted yet another sphere away from its protective cardboard holder for a closer look. This was the start of my education in this specialized art.

Whole worlds are inside a glass dome. Glass rods are cut, bundled together, and heated into molten glass. For certain paperweights, the molten glass bundles are reborn into what's called millefiori, a thousand flowers under a crystal glass dome that has been fired and shaped around them. In my hand, one palm-sized paperweight, shaped like a large mushroom cap, captured "a thousand flowers," and I clicked the light on my cellphone to examine it. Glass flowers that were the size of cut scallion tips had layers like scallions, colors surrounded by other colors, white on the outside, red, then pink, in clusters. Various shades of green and white in one flower cluster surrounded a tiny graphic of twins, the Zodiac sign of Gemini was the pistil, the center of the floral burst that was one of over a hundred colorful clusters. Looking closely, even without added magnification, I could spot the signs of the Zodiac scattered under the dome amid the millefiori. As I would return one paperweight to its resting place and pick up another, I began to examine the underside base of the weights. I saw inscriptions identifying Murano, the Venetian glass, Baccarat, the historic French glassworks, and other individual designer names. A few paperweights were created with pedestals formed from the same blown glass as their domes. A few were opaque, solid waves of color, veins of design culminating in a marbleized many-hued ball. I had to remind myself that the solid circle I was holding was actually glass, not painted plastic or stone.

All this beauty must have been buried in this closet for decades. Peter had died in 1996. Our discovery was taking place in 2018. The paperweights might have been with Peter in his house in Philadelphia and brought back after his death, or they could have been stored here the whole time. Whatever had been the trajectory of this collection, I was the accidental archivist bringing them back from obscurity; no longer would they be buried treasures left inside a closet. However, once again I was faced with the question of what kind of collectors lived in this house. There were no origin notes, no documentation about the age of the paperweights, who made them, and where. None of the dates embossed on the pieces themselves went beyond 1980. Although the flat "Peter's" boxes had individual compartments for each paperweight, the boxes themselves had been hidden in a closet, much the way Peter's life had been sadly hidden in a closet too.

While others may have a life goal of shaping a career, making money, or finding love, Peter sought originality. The wood-like, egg-shaped wasp nest hanging from the ceiling in his childhood bedroom was only one indication of what I considered his unusual interests. He did not watch television or follow pop culture. He seemed perfectly suited to a different century, perhaps the Victorian era. A frock coat and peg-top trousers would fit his style and manner. His taste ran to classical composers. Even as a preteen, Peter attempted Chopin on his accordion, the first musical instrument I remembered him playing. The accordion was still there in his room. I had hit the tip of my right foot on a large luggage-type case. Then I saw that it was not one case but two, one on top of another. I had stumbled upon two accordions, one black, one red, in separate velour-lined cases. The accordions' bellows were dried out, cracked, and shrunken. I could still recall the weight of the black one on my shoulders.

"Go ahead, Eileen, see how you like it," Peter said, as he lifted the black accordion straps on my shoulders and fastened them across my back. We were about thirteen years old at the time. The instrument was heavy and awkward, and I had no idea where to put my fingers to make it create music. I could barely stand.

Peter laughed. "Here, I'll show you," he said as he removed the accordion from my shoulders, professionally slid the straps onto his own, and played a polka. Music would become his life and career, but at first, it was just a contender. Amid the objects in his bedroom, a tall, professional Bausch & Lomb microscope stood out, and alongside it, as if waiting to be examined, was an assortment of glass slides containing insects and fossils. Musical instruments and laboratory tools revealed his dual interest in both music and science.

Four diverse personalities created the many diverse objects in this house, and identifying who was attached to which ones was slowly becoming easier. Each possession granted me a greater understanding, a greater ability to climb my family tree. Those objects I could attribute to Peter were more intellectual in nature. He had graduated in 1967 with a major in biology from MacMurray College in Jacksonville, Illinois. Yet during his college days, he was also a member of the American Guild of Organists and performed as the piano and organ accompanist of the college's choir. Sheet music, the works of Rachmaninoff, Chopin, Debussy, were jammed into a bookshelf built along one wall. Other shelves housed dozens of vintage books such as *Annual of Scientific Discovery*, in editions for various nineteenth-century years, *Relativity* by Albert Einstein, *Larousse Medical Illustre*. Classical music, historical science—these were the pieces of a person left behind. Nothing modern. These were Peter. A photo of him posing with an assortment of vintage clocks showed that he involved himself in his father's passion, and with the paperweights labeled in his name, he clearly participated in his mother's immersion in glass art. He was keeping each parent happy, showing equal interest within his family. This was my cousin, the conscientious objector to the Vietnam War.

I watched him walking toward me in a hallway of the Thomas Jefferson University Medical College in Philadelphia, where he was doing community service in microbiology research in lieu of fighting in the rice paddies—a lean, six-foot-tall professional in a sunlit white lab coat. With his broad smile and black-rimmed glasses, he looked typecast in the role of peaceful professor. We were not that far away from college, still in our twenties. I thought Peter would probably remain a scientific researcher throughout his life. He seemed so comfortable in the laboratory. Instead, although he stayed in Philadelphia, he created a career in music, playing the organ and harpsichord as musical director of Old Pine Street Church, and for secular events. I did not know on the day I visited him at Thomas Jefferson that my interesting cousin was a gay man and that a terrible disease would kill him, as it did many gay men, when he was only fifty-one years old. The dried-out accordions at my feet were reminders of him and our childhood, but they were also relics of the days when these instruments were more popular and commonplace among young people. Looking at them now, they seemed as archaic as the Dead Sea Scrolls. Yet I was still alive and I could feel and write the history.

The paperweights were a sign that Peter was also a collector, but so far, I had no indication that he harbored a hoarding habit. A fifth 30-cubic-yard dumpster arrived in the driveway. It was February 2018, and we had already filled and hauled away four of these monsters. Why were the rooms still filled with debris and all sorts of objects? Although we had donated or stored countless items, trashed tons of garbage mixed with possessions of little or no value, and sometimes even thrown out items we should have kept, the house was far from empty. Was I existing in an optical illusion where there really was more open space within the rooms than I could see or feel? No, the CleanUppers, the repairmen, Ellen, all agreed that although we were indeed on our fifth dumpster, the house remained packed. I was not losing my mind.

The storeroom that was Peter's room held boxes and bags of plastic Japanese mini-toys—tiny anime characters, gremlins, superheroes, and animals. These were leaning against, on top of, and sometimes underneath boxes of commercial Christmas ornaments and the crafts: the wires, glues, glitters, ribbons, beads, little baskets, tiny teddy bears, and basic glass balls—all there for creating personal Christmas ornaments. Signs of Christmas, like the miniature plastic Christmas trees in the living room, were throughout the house. In Peter's space, these were related to Bob, who left notes about how many palm crosses he made for Easter and the number of ornaments he created for his church's thrift shop to sell during the Christmas season. At first, I had thought that the holidays, especially the Christmas holidays, must have brought so much happiness to Bob that he found ways to keep Christmas close every day, but then I considered the opposite. Perhaps the holidays were not a happy time for him, and he wanted to give himself and those who received his handmade ornaments a pleasure he had missed earlier in life. Whatever was driving him led to the artifacts of Christmas in abundant supply throughout the house.

    I was drawn back to the beauty of Peter's paperweights, the uniqueness of each one. In keeping with this house of time, with clocks and watches throughout, one diamond-shaped paperweight, of Lucite rather than glass, contained a small clock face without hands. The wheels that are the gears of a timepiece singularly floated in the airy space of the diamond above the numbered clock face. They were like stars around the moon in a night sky. At some point, before the house would be put on the market, we knew that we would try to sell valued objects at auction. Certainly, these paperweights would be included in such a sale. They had been saved for decades under Peter's name. In a small or larger way, they were part of who Peter was. I knew at that moment that I would photograph and document them. I would also keep a few as reminders of my gentle cousin whose parents, Mike and Marie, could never openly admit that their son was a gay man.

    Peter lived with his own beauty in protective packaging, much like the glass artistry in my hands. I envisioned him walking with his mother at one of those open-air flea markets that are so ubiquitous in the southern farmland areas of New Jersey where pickup trucks abound. Eight-foot folding tables line up to make a 24-foot stretch of surface with the leftover items from estates: flatware, clocks, serving dishes, candleholders, ashtrays, teapots, salt and pepper shakers.

Maybe, perhaps, between a ceramic soap dish and a hurricane glass oil lamp, Peter reached down and retrieved an exquisite glass millefiori paperweight which Marie had spied first and pointed out to him. There had to have been some reason that the three boxes of paperweights were only labeled as "Peter's." He had to have had a hand in bringing the collection together.

I remembered Marie's *Reasons For Collecting*, which included

Try to teach your children early to appreciate quality etc.—Keeps them out of trouble.

Some of the paperweights were marked and dated in the 1960s and 1970s but since a number of them had no dates, I could not tell how historic or recently made they all might be. Throughout the 1960s and 1970s Peter was in high school, college, and then out in the world. The beautiful paperweights, whenever they became a collection, could have been the result of Marie's drive to imprint her sense of "quality" onto her children.

With a little digging, I discovered that there is neuroscience showing that the same area of the brain that's activated when beauty is perceived is also linked to collecting behavior. The possibility that the pleasure that comes from, for example, experiencing the beauty in a garden of yellow roses could match the pleasure elicited from the acquisition of objects might explain why Marie and possibly Mike, Bob, and Peter too, were caught up in collecting items. They could have been neurologically charged and excited by the accumulation of objects, and this stimulation, when combined with their sense of the beauty of their acquisitions—well, what joy! The collecting of pretty things like Peter's paperweights must have made them feel good, but at some point, things changed. For someone in this family, or for everyone in this family, collecting turned an unmapped corner into hoarding.

I set aside the flat boxes of gorgeous glass paperweights and began to look into what else was in the conglomeration of assorted packing and file boxes in Peter's bedroom. Set inside a large canvas shopping bag, I found stamp albums, the kind of fat books that hold time-honored stamp collections. *The Crown World Stamp Album*, 12" × 12" and over 1,000 pages on which black-and-white images of stamps from every country on the planet were laid out as templates over which the actual stamps of color were to be secured. Only a few of the 1,000 pages were completely filled. This heavy book was on top of another, *The New World Wide Postage Stamp Album*, 12" × 12" but with 350 pages, it was one-third of the heft of the *Crown* album. Previously, Ellen and I had discovered letter-size envelopes holding canceled stamps, stored within larger manila envelopes that surfaced unexpectedly. One manila envelope was beside a box of hats, for example. Then there were the stamps in folders safely kept in dresser drawers, Mike's and Marie's and Bob's dresser drawers. (Peter's room had no dresser.) Were the stamps kept for their artistry or historic relevance, or because my relatives felt the stamps held monetary worth? This was my own rhetorical question to myself. I knew better. My massive emptying of the rooms that held the lives in this house had made me a student of hoarding and collecting. I reminded myself that intellectual reason did not have to play a part in the saving of anything. Objects can be thought of warmly, as good friends or treasured family members, and no monetary value can ever match their emotional worth.

I lifted a carton of antique toy soldiers from a pile and carefully maneuvered a wide box that held a Tiffany-style leaded glass lampshade of a skyscape sunset—blue, green, yellow, and orange, just beyond an emerald body of water, a shoreline, and in the distance, dark pines. The lead overlay on the glass skyscape was a canopy of treetops. Don't let me break this, I said to myself as I repositioned the boxed lampshade just enough inches to my left to allow me to reach over to a large shopping bag that held what looked like, yes, it was, family photos. This was the collection that mattered most to me. Its emotional value was enormous and its worth, priceless, but only to me.

I pulled from the bag something else: an aged brown photo album with frayed edges and brittle paper pages the color of mud. Inside the cover, on a hardened blank page, was printed in what looked like black fountain pen ink: Peter Michael Stukane. The birth and early childhood of my cousin were between the covers of this book, so fragile and delicate that I felt it could crack apart in my hands. And there we are: Peter and I together in New York City. We're sitting in front of a Christmas tree as one-year-olds, at each other's birthday parties every year from age one to six, playing in the snow on fire escapes, on tricycles in Tompkins Square Park, running in Central Park, our parents hovering in the background. Our younger siblings, Peter's brother Bob and my sister Ellen, begin to appear in photos with us. I hug the vintage album to my chest. I love this object. It validates the connection to family that I have been feeling every moment I have been in this house. If what I feel for this album is anything like the emotions my relatives experienced when they looked at, or touched, the objects in their lives, then I have an understanding of how deeply difficult parting with any items, material though they are, had to be.

I called Ellen over to turn the album pages with me. She appeared with a folder she had found within Mike's documents in a desk drawer in the master bedroom. The papers related to the sale of Peter's home in Philadelphia. Mike was the owner of the house; Peter lived rent-free. Along with the appraisal and notes about the sale of the house were photos of the premises, the rooms. I reflexively covered my mouth with my right hand as a slight nausea rose from my stomach through my chest. We turned over picture after picture of rooms that looked like the ones we were standing in. Garbage strewn everywhere, boxes, papers, food, books, and a narrow goat path between the detritus. This was Peter's home. This was how Peter lived. As if on cue, Ellen and I spoke the same words together: "Oh my God, he was a hoarder too." The genetics of the situation once more rose before us. Whether hoarding disorder was in our genes, or whether this behavior in our family was the result of external trauma, depression, or family dynamics, the photos showed that it had spared no one who had lived in this house.

5

Bob's Christmas Every Day

The brothers, Peter and Bob, were more similar in nature than I had realized. Their left-behind possessions revealed different but parallel, scientific and artistic interests—Peter's objects were connected to biology and music; Bob's items aligned with his focus on computer technology and painting. Now, with the discovery of photos of clutter from inside Peter's home, my cousins Peter and Bob were drawing another parallel, this time to those historic hoarder brothers, Homer and Langley Collyer.

Even though they lived apart in different states and towns, both Peter and Bob existed in self-made fortresses of stuff that kept the outside world truly outside. Although hoarding disorder (HD) is known to run in families, I had thought that Peter, living on his own in Philadelphia, had been spared. Perhaps his Chromosome 14 gave him a compelling genetic connection. Perhaps both brothers shared this gene.

Researchers at Johns Hopkins University School of Medicine linked Chromosome 14 to hoarding disorder among people with Obsessive-Compulsive Disorder (OCD), who also happened to be in families with two or more members who hoarded. In addition to this possible genetic link, a 2017 review of the causes of HD from researchers at San Diego State University/University of California made the point that in a study of seventy-one older people (ages 60–85) with HD, almost 50 percent of them said they had a mother with hoarding tendencies. Marie considered herself a collector but she hardly behaved like one. Usually a collector displays, buys, and sells. Marie hid her collections, bought, but never sold. I could see her having "hoarding tendencies."

I did not need further validation. I could look at the situations with both brothers and see that hoarding disorder was in the family. Bob, however, had more room for massive accumulation in his three-bedroom childhood home—which held the possessions of four family members—than Peter did at his Philadelphia address.

In the house, I put myself in Bob's shoes, became him, and stood on the narrow footpath created by shoulder-high piles of boxes and debris from the living room into the dining room. From a vantage point where the two rooms met, I scanned the confined space and took in the vast array of objects in an area of about 650 square feet.

My gaze fell upon the two-foot-high, hand-painted Asian porcelain lamp base resting on a side table next to a sofa that was buried under trash. The lamp was striking with its mostly yellow and russet colors of flowers bordering an image of an opened Japanese rice paper screen with a kimonoed woman seated in the foreground. By now I knew that all things Asian in the house were chosen by Marie, so this object was hers. Imagining that I was looking through Bob's eyes, I saw the light from this lamp shining on poignant memories of a mother gone too soon. Still on the path, with a slight turn of my head, I caught a glance of Mike's beloved wall clock that was no longer ticking, the clock's pendulum weights on the floor. So this is how it goes, I thought. A son's defiance against the father who controlled time is to make time stop.

An empathy for Bob and an understanding of family life in this house were seeping into my consciousness. A sense of compassion, which I never could have predicted I would experience on the first day I walked through the front door, was deepening as I sorted and touched each person's possessions. Every day, inanimate objects intensified in their importance, told their stories, and claimed their places as vibrant vessels of people's lives. Of course, this aliveness made final decisions more difficult. We marked individual U-Haul boxes: "Keep, Auction, Throw Out, Donate, Not Sure (when we needed more time to decide whether to throw out or a save an object)." Declaring the fate of each item could be quick and easy or drawn-out and wrenching. Somewhere nearby, the ghost of Bob nodded.

Bob signed his artwork Bobjon. An oil painting of his, partially obscured by cardboard boxes, hung on a wall behind the undetectable, buried-under-refuse sofa in the living room. A golden image rose from the solid black of the painted canvas. I had been captivated in the past by the glimmering of a turreted tower rising from a rocky landmass of gold. The glowing tower and its base were unmoored, floating, starlike, through a black void. At the pointy tip of the tower's spire, a golden bird perched. Most of Bob's paintings were abstractions, shapes painted over monochromatic backgrounds, which Ellen and I found in his bedroom. This realistic painting was different, an image beautiful and hopeful, a golden tower resembling a tall protective lighthouse at night, a symbol of safe passage.

I knew the painting had hung in that living room for years, having seen its glow throughout at least four decades of visits. The glittering golden tower seemed a symbol of hope, but the black shadowless void took up a much greater space. Did Bob live in the darkened emptiness? Or in the tower with the high-flying bird that could take off at any moment? Or was he the bird? Letters, notebooks, and journals unearthed in Bob's room exposed the emotional tug-of-war that he battled with while living in a family of withdrawn emotions. Mike, Marie, Peter, his parents and brother were collectors (and in the case of Mike and Marie, likely borderline hoarders) who treasured their discovered items perhaps more than they did each other. In this environment, I could see how Bob might naturally turn to objects for solace. They were cared for more than the people in his childhood home. Hoarding disorder can start in the teen years, but as far as I knew, Bob did not comfort himself with things until he was an older adult.

A younger Bob wanted to experiment and flee from his surroundings. His early notebooks, many containing his poetry in his own handwriting, remained on his bedroom shelves for us to find in our hunt for answers. A typical excerpt, written in his twenties, reveals a young man who is searching for a connection:

> I have not much to offer
> And perhaps I am Insane
> Am I mad to want
> To help someone to smile
> To care
> To share the things I find
> Along the path that some call Life
> To strive to see the rainbow
> And the star
> I sit alone again
> The compass badly shaken
> And not in synch with time
> What hand had I
> In the course of things
> Was it the time and place
> Or me

To read Bob's words, to feel his longing for a meaningful, personal relationship was heartbreaking. Discovered letters from women revealed that he experienced sexual intimacies, but he never succeeded in creating a lifetime partnership. "I have not much to offer," the first line of his poem, may be a clue to his future hoarding disorder and his aloneness. Psychologists who study hoarding behavior have learned that people who lack confidence in their self-worth are often the same people who hoard. Do objects offer a sense of importance? Researchers continue to search for an answer to that question.

After two years at Clemson University in Tennessee, where he was majoring in architecture, Bob transferred to Hiram College in Ohio, majored in painting, and worked toward a Bachelor of Fine Arts degree. He painted and even exhibited work at the school, but he dropped out before graduation and began to roam. An emotional search for self-identity took him on an actual journey.

In the early 1970s, he fit right into a nomadic counterculture that broke away from traditional nine-to-five workdays. It was easy to be on the road then because hippie communes, popping up in different states across the country, embraced wandering strangers. The "Turn On/Tune In/Drop Out" words of Timothy Leary, a Harvard (from which he was fired) psychologist and popular proponent of the use of psychedelic drugs like LSD (Lysergic Acid Diethylamide), inspired young people to explore their psyches through drugs and find new lifestyles. Bob, uncertain and seeking, perfectly fit the profile of a Leary acolyte. Correspondence from friends mentioned his drug use but not his choice of drug. While the use of hallucinogenic drugs was not unusual for his age and the times, what was unusual was that Bob did not seem to mature beyond those days. Friends continued to pen long handwritten letters to him, encouraging Bob to find a purpose. I found letters from Marie, who sent Bob money and asked him to please come home.

The turning point came in 1980 when Mike and Marie traveled to California to bring their son back to the East Coast. Bob, still traveling, was assaulted while he was staying in a motel. The family story was that he was pistol-whipped and lost consciousness. Authorities notified Mike and Marie. After years of exploring, Bob was back in the New Jersey home of his childhood, where he would continue to live until the day of his death in 2016.

Psychologists cite trauma and PTSD as underlying issues that can lead to hoarding. Now I was realizing that Bob had a basketful of situations that are named as probable causes of hoarding behavior. He had a distant father, a diminished sense of self-worth, a lack of direction, and trauma from an assault. A psychologist who treated Bob in 1982 and who wrote up her analysis—one that was kept in a dining room sideboard—diagnosed him as feeling persecuted, victimized, and angry at authority figures. In addition to whatever neurological damage may have resulted from his assault, the therapist concluded that Bob harbored an Explosive Personality and Paranoia. Her recommendation was that he continue to undergo psychotherapy to help him revise his life story of perceived victimization. There is no evidence that this course was taken. Instead, Bob seemingly decided that objects were easier to live with than people.

However, he did return to school, attended two different two-year colleges, and became certified in computer programming, which I realized, was just another interaction with an object. Eventually, he was able to earn an income as a freelance tech consultant, but he never became self-supporting. He remained living with his parents who nurtured the objects I was in the throes of discovering. Over time, following the examples set by his parents, Bob cosseted himself with lots of stuff of his own, eventually outmatching Mike and Marie in the quantity of possessions.

Stacks of *Model Railroad News* magazines from years past teetered asymmetrically on barely balanced cardboard boxes in the living room. At the start of my mission to solve the mystery of Bob's death, his friend Ted had told me that whenever Bob's pain was under control, he would make an effort to drive to, and spend a day at, any model train show on the calendar in New Jersey. According to Ted, Bob loved going to the shows and buying assorted model train cars. This was one of Bob's pleasures, but with all the garbage and clutter, no open space existed for laying out model railroad tracks, tunnel overpasses, stations, and villages in miniature. I also was unable to locate where the purchased trains might be. They were not near the magazines. Smoggy clouds rose up as I disturbed the settled dust on whatever I touched. I lifted boxes, pushed bags of cleaning supplies and paper towels aside, and finally gave up. When I could not find any model trains, I admitted defeat, left the living room, and returned to the master bedroom.

Boxes of VHS tapes were set out in columns spread across the queen-size bed. This room where Mike and Marie had slept was now a collection site for random objects. I worked with one of our CleanUppers to move the boxes aside, and as we shifted things, at least six brand-new, foot-long, narrow rectangular boxes of green and red surfaced. Visible beneath the see-through plastic windows of the packaging were individual model train cars, boxcars, tank cars, and engines, in HO gauge. Hidden under folded drapery fabric and near a plastic container of sewing supplies, separate boxes of model train accessories, tracks, and even some greenery, miniature trees, and bushes emerged. I had believed what Ted had told me, so I felt victorious.

In the neighborhood, barely two miles away, about a five-minute drive from Bob's home, the Toy Train Emporium must have attracted him. After twenty-two years in business, the Emporium closed in

2018 while Ellen and I were spending our time in Cherry Hill. With Bob's interest in model trains and the Toy Train Emporium so close by, I envisioned him visiting the store often, if only to seek childlike refuge from his troubled adult existence.

I do not recall either of my cousins in their childhoods, playing with trains on tracks that would have been set up by Mike, those circular tracks on the floor, laid out near a Christmas tree by so many fathers. No found holiday photos show Peter and Bob as boys with trains. The sleuth in me saw the trains as evidence of how Bob, who was in physical pain and emotional turmoil, eased his suffering. The trains, the ornaments, and the many toys I would find, brought Christmas into the chaos every day. Still in the master bedroom, I could feel the twelve grimy nutcracker dolls staring at me while standing at attention on the top of Mike's dresser. Every room was touched by something Christmassy. In addition to those dozen nutcracker dolls in the bedroom, the miniature plastic Christmas trees in the living room, the shiny colors of Christmas balls surfacing throughout the house like wildflowers in a field, all were telling me something... but what?

Children's toys were in Peter's former bedroom. Collections of antique toy soldiers and bags of plastic Japanese mini-toys—tiny anime characters, gremlins, superheroes, animals—were leaning against, on top of, and sometimes underneath boxes of commercial Christmas ornaments and, again, the crafts, the wires, glues, glitters, ribbons, beads, little baskets, tiny teddy bears, basic glass balls, all materials that Bob used to make his Christmas ornaments. I was beginning to think that Christmas must have brought Bob so much childlike happiness that he found ways to keep the holiday alive all the time, although he clearly went overboard.

Knowing my interest in learning why people over-accumulate objects, a friend connected me with Deacon Laverne S. Williams

CSW, director of the PEWS (Promoting Emotional Wellness and Spirituality) program of The Mental Health Association in New Jersey. She had a different, revelatory take on what might have been happening with Bob. Her involvement in workshops such as the 16-week Buried in Treasures workshop—"for people who tend to have too much stuff"—had given her a firsthand look into hoarding disorder. She made me aware that what I thought were Bob's attempts to hold onto joyful times were possibly just the opposite. "It could be that holidays were not a happy time for him, and 'that's why I want them, and I want them now'. There are so many layers," says Deacon Williams. "It could be 'I'm going to acquire these things and maybe I'll give them to someone so they don't have to experience what I did'. It could be many things when you ask someone 'What is the feeling you have about objects that you've purchased? Why did you want them so badly?'"

The menu of motivational options scrambled my previously clear-eyed assessments. The Christmas Every Day environment, which I saw as Bob's strongest strategy for keeping depression at bay, may not have been driven by his reliving of Happy Holidays with family. Bob may have been self-soothing, giving himself the pleasure of Christmas that he lacked from family, a joy he longed for but did not receive. Or was he fashioning Christmas ornaments for others to share a jolly remembered past?

I had to expand my thinking. During my time in the house, I had come to perceive Bob as a man in charge of his territory. He did what he wanted when he wanted. If he had an urge to leave that opened carton of Ritz crackers on the living room floor, then that's what he did. He was in control! My blindness was that I did not consider multiple aspects, a fuller range, of his personality. Although he might have had no qualms about his unsanitary surroundings—stifling and jam-packed—and he might have, deep within, seen himself as a victim, he still might have tried to bring happiness to others. He experienced a number of the life situations that can lead to hoarding—a distant father, a diminished sense of self-worth, trauma from an assault. All this, to me, meant that his persona—like the personas of so many who suffer from hoarding disorder—deserved a deeper exploration.

Father Jeffrey Kirk, at the time pastor of the neighboring Grace Episcopal Church, remembered Bob as always showing up to tune the carillon bells every Christmas season. The carillon had been donated by Mike and Marie, so Bob had a close family connection to the church. Father Kirk recalled Bob looking ashen and thin but still appearing on schedule. The pastor also spoke about the crosses made from palm leaves that Bob had crafted and donated to the church for distribution on Palm Sundays, the week before Easter, and his original Christmas ornaments, the ones he created for the church thrift shop's holiday sales.

I had held Bob's crosses and handmade ornaments, examining them carefully. Some of his personally crafted ornaments were still in boxes, ready for a trip to the church's thrift shop. A tiny bear in a beaded basket was held by golden threads onto a gold Christmas ball cleverly ringed with lines of beaded jewelry chain, a hook at the top guaranteeing this creation could decorate a pine tree branch—here was an original handcrafted holiday hot air balloon carrying its little teddy bear passenger. A variation on the theme of Christmas ball as hot air balloon appeared in an assortment of boxed works. Bob had self-identified as an artist in his college days when he painted abstract canvases. These ornaments were his final works of art. I began to look at the enormity of crafting supplies throughout the house; more glitter, beads, wires, and glues than one person could use in a lifetime, and dozens of boxes of new Christmas balls, unopened sparkles of light and color in every room. A testament to one man's desire to have more and more? Or a fear that there may not be enough?

Since people who hoard usually allow few visitors into their homes, it is difficult to pin down how many people in the United States live with—and successfully hide—their hoarding disorder. The "Hoarders" TV series told viewers that nineteen million US citizens shared the condition, but psychologists researching this behavior estimate that, on average, about 5 percent of the population, or approximately sixteen million Americans, are affected. Among those millions of men and women, there must be countless individual strategies for coping with the loneliness and the fears that cause the hoarding to exist.

In the book *So Much Stuff*, author and archaeologist Chip Colwell makes the point that "The desire for things goes back to the first stone cutting tool. . . . the first sculptures, weavings, houses, and clothes were made precisely because they were craved, coveted because of their function or for the wonder, beauty, or meaning they inspired." It seemed that Bob lived with that desire in the extreme. Two boxes of Christmas balls were not enough. He needed twenty. I also saw Bob standing in as the protector of his parents' collections, the caretaker of the objects they prized. Discarding even one of Marie's collected pieces might feel as if he were removing not just a memory of his mother, but actually removing her. She was still in the room with her things—even I felt that. With Marie's possessions present, her taste and style all around, she existed in the atmosphere. She was still there.

A sampling of poems Bob penned in a spiral notebook surprised me by revealing more of his inner life.

> Driving through valleys
> A mind full of dreams
> A soul full of pain

Watching the red light,
The yellow, and the green,
Life is the total
Is it all that it seems?
Shivering with cold
Drifting in thought
Feeling so empty
Lost and alone
To sleep and dream
To be at peace for a while
Oh how I wish it would last

And another:
Upon the walls
Adorned with past experiences
Hang strings of hope
And a beautiful maze of red-brown
Once delegated to oblivion.

And one more:
Ribbons of white drift past
The magic box from which feelings flow
Beneath on a field of grey
The sun issues its pungent fragrance
Through the sky boundary
The snow drifts but it is warm within

The loneliness and yet the hopefulness in Bob's writing revealed his internal optimism. Seeing that he faced despair but did not surrender to it, I could no longer be upset with him for the environment he had created to survive. I knew that he was suffering relentless back pain from a 2004 car crash. His friend Ted had told me that his pain had left him in thrall to OxyContin. His doctor refilled prescription after prescription, month after month, year after year. The apparent combination of Bob's solitude and addiction, I believed, brought on his fatal heart attack. A deep sorrow filled me for what I remembered of him and the person he might have been.

A younger Bob had hope, he had poetry, and he had dreams. Bob left behind dozens of 3" × 5" notebooks filled with recipes, handwritten in block letters, not cursive. Cooking would have been impossible in the garbage-filled kitchen with no space to move, the insect- and maggot-filled refrigerator, the blackened oily burners on a stove with congealed grease stains on the oven door, the many plastic bags of refuse, and the garden hose resting among condiments on the floor. Standing in the memory of a once-inviting kitchen and turning the tiny notebook pages, I read lists of ingredients and instructions for the hope of making a vast assortment of dishes: buttermilk pancakes, perogi, gourmet soba, sausage, zucchini cakes, to name a few. Fantasy food conjured by a fantasy chef.

Saving recipes, it turns out, is not unusual among those who hoard. What else didn't I know? Throughout my year of trying to unravel the mysteries that the house held, I dove into all the information I could find about how the life and mind of someone who suffers from hoarding disorder works. In the book *Stuff, Compulsive Hoarding and the Meaning of Things* by Randy O. Frost and Gail Steketee, a passage about a woman whose kitchen, like Bob's, was buried in chaotic clutter, prompted me to shout, "Look at this!" into an empty room. I was alone at my desk. The authors, facing the same situation I was in, had reasoned: "The mere possession of the cookbooks and recipes allowed her to enjoy thinking about the image of herself cooking and to imagine a potential identity as a cook. . . . Her things represented dreams, not realities. Getting rid of the things meant losing the dreams." Ah, the dreams! I found Bob's printed calling card: Over the background of a five-point star, it read: "Bobjon Builder of Dreams and Things."

Dreams are not objects, but I was realizing that dreams and desires were crucial to the accumulation. Bob expressed his inner conflict best in the lines of his poetry: Driving through valleys/A mind full of dreams/ A soul full of pain—words that described the duality of his personality but also his surroundings. The recipes that filled his notebooks were never going to be roasted, baked, broiled, or sauted but they must have given him a mental escape from his loneliness and depression.

The amassing of model trains and toys, and at least twenty different versions of Chinese Checkers plus other marble games, was a retreat into a fantasy childhood. Then, of course, there was his "Happy Holiday" paraphernalia, which allowed him to hold onto his "Builder of Dreams" identity as he crafted and painted ornaments. The more he experienced pleasure from certain possessions like the trains, toys, and Christmas decorations, the more he must have been trying to increase his joy. He bought more trains, more toys, more holiday items. He clung to his dreams, attempting to make them real.

On the other hand, he ignored real-life situations. Perhaps he thought he could deal with the daily issues of life later on. No opening the mail. Ten years of sealed envelopes and flyers grew into a mountainous pile that threatened to avalanche onto the dining room floor. (Dividend checks from Mike's investments were continuously surfacing as Ellen and I laboriously examined every piece of paper that we had removed from the Cherry Hill house to hers.) Bob allowed rotting food to continue rotting. His supply of toilet paper and paper towels could meet the needs of a small hotel for a year, but he never cleaned. Bob's back injury, which occurred a year before Mike died, might have made it harder for him to do anything physical, but repairmen could have helped if only he had called them.

The cracked and broken toilet tank in a bathroom where no water flowed from any faucets might have been made whole again. Instead, in this sad bathroom, empty cigarette cartons carpeted the floor, a sagging shower rod was crowded with clothes on hangers—flannel shirts, pants, a suit, but also glittery silver and gold Christmas balls sparkled in boxes heaped high in the tub. It happened over and over that just as I'd feel myself sliding into despair, a burst of beauty or something of pleasure would lift me up, change my mood. This is how Bob must have lived, sometimes low and depressed, and other times energized and elated. Mixed among the bathroom floor's ripped cigarette cartons were flower catalogs offering bulbs of loveliness—tulips, lilies, narcissi.

Ellen and I were filling our sixth 30-cubic yard dumpster. We sighed over Bob's oil paintings, facing them as we had with so many objects that vibrated with the energy of the person who possessed them. Solomonic decisions had to be reached about what would be dispensed to the dumpster and forever forgotten, or spared, as a remembrance, a donation, or an auction item. I felt a hoarder's dilemma about what to keep and what to throw away because, as I had come to understand, for someone who hoards, discarding a loved one's belongings feels like a removal of that person, the memory of that person, from the world. I would be disposing of Bob's artistry, a visual representation of his inner being. I wished I were not in this situation.

My mind wandered. Although everything I had researched told me that trying to change the behavior of someone who hoards is extremely difficult, I drifted into thought about what I might have done, how I might have been able to help my relatives if I had known about the hoarding done in secret, behind that closed front door. Ellen's elbow nudged me back to the present to decide the fate of Bob's artwork. Eventually, the brown and beige abstract, which to me resembled a fried egg, went to the dumpster. The living room's golden tower, glowing in the blackest of nights, was marked for auction. I gave each of the ten painted canvases thought and attention, as if Bob, the artist, were standing with me. In his hope and in his pain, which I had come to feel from everything he had left behind, I liked to think that he was guiding the destiny of his possessions.

6

Effie and Jacob
Family Secrets Revealed

In the small chest in the dining room, the one with the drawer of family photos that popped out during our earliest days in the house, in a corner of that same drawer was an ancient brass-etched teacup from China. A teacup in a drawer did not surprise me. Unrelated objects were on shelves and in drawers throughout the house. It was something settled in the bottom of the cup that proved unexpected: a gold signet ring, initials: AM. I knew immediately that this graced the finger of my grandmother, Agafia Mosendzova, my father's mother. It perfectly fit the ring finger of my right hand. I felt an immediate, somewhat mystical, connection. Our hands must have been similar.

As with so many objects in the house, this ring might have been lost if we had not moved as slowly and carefully as we did. Other items in the cup: a few paper clips, a couple of buttons, a man's large H signet ring, probably worn by Marie's father (surname "Hydukurtz," changed to "Hyde" by Marie), three unadorned rings of copper and brass, two small vintage lapel pins, one for Girls Friendly Society and another, blue enamel, a half-inch in diameter with mysterious letters—The N.G. of A.—printed across an image of open scissors, bordered by a spool of thread and a thimble. This pin with the illustrated scissors surely had something to do with my grandmother's occupation as a seamstress. Such an assortment of objects somehow became mingled together in the cup with that best find of all, the gold AM ring that now encircled my finger.

My teacup discovery occurred at the time I felt that the house was performing a self-cleansing. The interior water pipes in the house had frozen due to a mistake by a helper who turned the attic fan on a reverse draft. Ellen had called the town to turn off the water main supply to the house until the temperature inside could climb. As the rooms warmed up, the water was turned back on, and that's when the cleansing began. Pipes that were never supposed to hold frozen water had cracked. When the heat rose, water thawed in the pipes, shot through those cracks, and ultimately, through the walls. Indeed, a wet spray touched my shoulder a few times. I could not help but feel I was experiencing a kind of baptism by the house.

A rebirth taking place through the walls offered an amusing metaphor that I shared with our hired helpers. However, the house was also about to give birth to something important: the foundational story of my father's family. When, finally, with enough debris removed, there was space to open dresser drawers in the master bedroom, I happened upon aging folders of documents that told truths I had never heard. Mixed in with records Mike kept for managing the maintenance of his pocket watches, wristwatches, and clocks were papers of another kind, archived information that would expose hidden secrets. It was almost as if placing my grandmother's ring on my finger had opened a Pandora's Box of family history.

My paternal grandmother Agafia, who changed her name to Effie, died when I was seven years old, but now the house was bringing her back to life. The oft-repeated family history was that my father's father, my grandfather, had died when my father was two years old.

My father Edward, better known as Ed, and his brother Mike were raised in New York City by their hard-working single mother who, like so many female laborers in the 1920s, 1930s, and 1940s, became a contracted worker in sewing factories. I grew up understanding from my father that his mother went wherever jobs needed to be filled. She was always moving around. She might be sewing blouses in a Garment District workshop one week and hemming drop cloths somewhere in Brooklyn during the next.

Within one manila envelope in a dresser drawer of Mike's, among socks left in place since his passing in 2005, a record from the ship that brought Effie to the United States gave me the beginning of her back story, which started in 1913. That was the year she emigrated from the Russian Empire, although her hometown was actually located within present-day Ukraine. No birth certificate exists to confirm her age, but from other found records, it seemed she was only sixteen years old when she undertook her solitary voyage as a third-class passenger on the ocean liner RMS Franconia. She had walked up the gangway of the Franconia in Liverpool, England. At docking, she walked down that same ramp and stepped onto New York City soil in the United States of America. The day was April 7, 1913. The tall, blue-eyed, sandy-haired teenager who spoke no English was completely alone in her new country, having left a Russia that would enter the First World War one year later, in 1914.

No notes or documents explained her motivation to leave her homeland, or whether she was an only child or one of several siblings. Questions cropped up in my mind: Where did she go when she left the dock? Was someone from New York's Russian community meeting her? Did she find her way to the Russian Immigrant Home on East 14th Street in Manhattan? My father and uncle spoke of her as "White Russian," more Menshevik, less radical and middle-class, than the working-class Bolshevik, so perhaps she had some money for lodging.

I will never know how Effie survived during her first few years in the city, but I would learn about other events in her later life. People who suffer from hoarding disorder often value an over-supply of single-category items like paper towels, or in Bob's case, Christmas balls, but they also save and protect important personal things. Bob saved his father's family history. Surprisingly, I found no documents that could tell me about his mother's family history. Perhaps they were kept by Marie's sister Olga.

Mike's drawers of documents helped define Effie's life, and later, her death in 1952. These documents, in effect hard copies of the past, changed what I had considered accurate family history. As with so much else that appeared in different rooms, corners, drawers, and boxes, other artifacts documenting the lives of my grandmother Effie and grandfather Jacob appeared in diverse areas. Like an archaeologist on a dig for remnants of the past, I carefully explored this house of hoarding disorder, this site of family fossils that fate had assigned me.

After emptying out further square footage in the master bedroom, I was able to open the drawers of a rolltop secretary desk that stood against a wall. More family history resided within the covers of soiled folders. Effie, still called Agafia Mosendzova at the time, married Jacob Stukane in 1916, three years after her arrival in America, when she was nineteen years old. Their certificate of marriage, long-untouched, was issued by the "Clerk of the Orphans Court of Philadelphia County, Pennsylvania" (which today is known as "The Court of Common Pleas, Orphan's Court Division"). Jacob was likely thirty-one or thirty-two, or perhaps twenty-nine when they were married. Different discovered documents state different years for his birth, but he was at least ten years older than Effie when he became her husband.

Jacob, whose birthplace was also within the borders of today's Ukraine, had crossed the Atlantic in 1911, sailing on the SS Cleveland from Hamburg to New York two years before Effie arrived. How Effie and Jacob met, what brought them to Philadelphia to wed, and then sent them back to New York City together to live, were vacant spaces in their stories. I tangled with more furniture drawers for clues. I searched as many as I could get to in bedroom dressers, the dining room sideboard, any table with a drawer. I wanted to unearth every piece of paper and photo so that nothing important would end up in a dumpster.

Effie gave birth to Mike in 1917 in Camden, New Jersey, not far from Philadelphia, and only 20 miles from the Cherry Hill, New Jersey house I was standing in, the house where he died. In 1920, three years after her first childbirth, Effie, now twenty-three years old, gave birth to my father, Edward, in New York City. The growing family lived on Lenox Avenue in New York City's Harlem, where Jacob worked as a furrier. I had known that my father's family had lived for a time in Harlem, but I knew little of my ancestral history. In recounting his roots, my father had told me that grandfather Jacob had died when he—my father—was two years old, but here is where the house started revealing discrepancies, family secrets, ones that would never have been known if there had been a mass discarding.

A copy of the New York City Census for 1920 lists Jacob and Effie as Jewish. Among the papers, I found Effie's membership in the Russian Orthodox Church. Both Mike and Ed were baptized Russian Orthodox (although my father converted to Catholicism in his teens and we, his family, were brought up as church-going Roman Catholics). Was the listed Jewish faith a census-taker's mistake, or did I have Jewish heritage? On Jacob's 1920 petition for citizenship, he lists Khmelnick (in present-day Ukraine) as his birthplace. A quick Google search of Khmelnick revealed it to be a historic Jewish community. Perhaps the census-taker was mistaken about Effie's religious background, but not about Jacob's. My roots were branching out in surprising directions.

I saw the curling edges of a folder under a yellow legal pad in a drawer of the secretary. In the folder was Effie's 1928 Petition for Citizenship. Filling in the required information on the form, Effie had written that Jacob had become a US citizen in 1923, a year after his supposed death in 1922. During her life, my father's presumed-to-have-been-widowed mother was, in fact, never a widow. My father's father was not deceased, as my father had been told. Effie and Jacob, and eventually Mike and his family, knew the truth, but they kept our family in the dark. Mike finally revealed Jacob's whereabouts to Ed a few months before Jacob's passing in 1960, but until then, everyone who lived in this house had continued to pretend that Jacob had died. Now, with found documents, I could piece together a scattershot tale of what had happened during the decades between my father's birth and Jacob's true death. I felt grateful to Bob for keeping ancestry documents intact. He was the last person alive in the house, and he could have done anything he wanted to with its contents. Bob saved everything.

The documents remained in their stashed corners, rumpled, somewhat discolored, but still there. I collected them from Mike's dresser, Marie's dresser, and from the secretary desk. I tried to order them chronologically, starting with Effie and Jacob's Certificate of Marriage in 1916. Of course, there were the birth certificates, Mike's from 1917 and Ed's from 1920. Once Jacob gained his citizenship in 1923, he disappeared from photographs and documents. He seemed to have fled the family. Supporting my father's stories of Effie's industriousness, employment booklets showed her laboring as a day contractor, sewing wherever she could get work.

I unfold a browning letter, papery frail, like a butterfly's wing. The letterhead stated: "Bureau of Police, City of Easton, Pennsylvania." The letter was sent in June 1930 to a New York City lawyer from the chief of police in Easton. The Chief was reporting that the police in Easton had been unable to locate Jacob at the address where he was supposed to be residing . . . "an officer called at the residence on two occasions and was unable to find either Stukane or anyone who had ever heard of him." Well, OK, he was supposed to be dead anyway. Since he was clearly alive, I now pictured him as a Deadbeat Dad running away from his responsibilities.

A few days after unfolding the letter to the Easton police, I discovered a warrant issued for Jacob's arrest in 1931, a year after the Easton search. Effie is the "Petitioner." The warrant was issued by the "Domestic Relations Court of the City of New York—Family Court." As I read the warrant, now a soft, yellowed sheet of paper, I saw that although there was an original warrant issued in 1931, what I am reading is a warrant twice-renewed, in 1935 and 1936. For child support? The fact that my father did not know his father was alive and apparently in Pennsylvania led me to think that support, rather than a custody battle, was the source of the warrant. As objects in the house, the chief of police letter, and the arrest warrant had already lasted about ninety years. The difficulty someone suffering from hoarding disorder has about throwing anything personal away had worked in my favor here. Precious objects of family history had been saved, ones that had exposed the hidden, truer story of my father's family of origin. Through decades, Effie and Mike had kept Jacob's existence a secret from their son and brother, my father Ed.

When Effie became a US citizen in 1933, twenty years after she stepped onto that dock in New York City, she legally changed her name from Agafia to Effie, a change officially typed on the back of her Certificate of Citizenship. As a citizen, she attempted to track down her estranged husband. Finally, in 1941, a divorce between Effie and Jacob was decreed "In the Court of Common Pleas of Northampton

County" in Pennsylvania. As I looked at the document of divorce, I realized that it was issued almost twenty years after Jacob had stopped being involved in the family he had helped create. Effie, who had remade herself as a "fake widow," was actually, and now officially, Effie, the "secret divorcee."

These decisions to cover up the truth meant that my nuclear family—my father, mother, and four of us siblings—were basing our origins on stories made of air. If I had never entered the house in Cherry Hill, I would have continued to be deceived about who knew what, and when. Truths were breaking out into the light, secrets were being exposed, because the four people who had lived in this house had refused to throw anything out. Also, aside from everything in it, the house itself was a secret. It was not the home I had been welcomed into in prior years, but a home I had been discouraged—by Bob—from visiting in recent years. Metaphorically, the house left by Bob was like a Russian Matryoska nesting doll, one large doll—the house of hoarding itself—holding many secrets in a series of smaller and smaller dolls that needed to be opened one by one.

I wanted to climb inside the minds of my relatives to learn what had motivated them to hide certain truths. From Michael Slepian, PhD's book *The Secret Life of Secrets*, I learned that a secret is not an action but an intention. In Dr. Slepian's words: "Whatever actions you take around keeping your secret, and whatever the context that surrounds that decision, what is common across all secrets is one thing: you intend for other people to not learn the information. This is what makes something a secret." The intention to withhold information—the foundation for secrets—was shared by my grandmother and my uncle, and apparently, by my aunt and cousins too.

On his 1937 application for Social Security, Jacob named the Eagle Fur Shop in Easton, Pennsylvania as his employer. His home address was in Phillipsburg, New Jersey. In 1960, when Ed was forty years old, his brother Mike told him he had met a man in a bar who was familiar with the name Stukane and had given him a lead to a man who lived in Phillipsburg, New Jersey. Since Effie had passed away in 1952, she was no longer alive at this time. Mike had recounted to Ed that he had tracked down this mysterious "Stukane," and the man was indeed Jacob, their father. Mike gave his brother an address and phone number, and Ed arranged a visit with Jacob.

The six of us—my father, mother, myself, and my three siblings—arrived at a dwelling of cement block walls and a roof of tin. As we approached the door of this ramshackle structure with an outhouse in view, a short, perhaps 5'6", crystal-blue-eyed man who strikingly resembled Mike opened the portal and welcomed us in. On his round face, he wore rimless glasses, and his combed-back sandy hair was thin but not gray. At 6'3", Ed looked down at this father of his with similar blue eyes. Then he took a step back so he would not loom over Jacob, who must have also been quite a bit shorter than the woman he married, the tall, posture-perfect Effie.

Ed was not motivated to connect more than casually with his estranged father. What compelled him to visit was a strong desire to show Jacob that, unlike the man who had abandoned him, Ed was a loving father. The most important people in his life were his wife and children, two girls and two boys, ages five to fifteen at the time.

We all stood side by side in the low-ceilinged dwelling that was basically one large room, with a bed, a table, a few chairs, and a six-foot-long, horizontal freezer filled with fur coats and assorted animal skins. Jacob tried to convince my mother to take a beaver coat home. She declined. He draped the coat over her shoulders. She more firmly declined. I had the sense that she wanted minimal contact with Jacob until she had a chance to hear his story and understand him. An opportunity for greater insight into the man would never occur, though. This would be the one and only time Ed would see his father.

It was an awkward meeting. My father asked why Jacob had abandoned his family, left his wife and children. Jacob did not offer a coherent answer. He responded in Russian, the language of my father's childhood, which Ed still understood: "You don't know what it was like to live with that woman," was his response, which my father later translated for us. However, I could tell by my father's pursed lips and furrowed brow when they were talking, that a strained and strange conversation was taking place.

A few months later, Jacob died. He was approximately seventy-five years old. The death certificate I later found in the folder in Mike's dresser listed the cause as uremia, basically kidney failure. My guess was that Mike must have known that Jacob was ill, perhaps at the end of his life, so he finally decided to tell his brother where his father could be found. Perhaps he wanted to unburden himself of his secret.

The objects left behind, the documents I had retrieved from furniture drawers, the police letter, arrest warrant, and divorce decree, were among Effie's belongings when she died of a sudden heart attack in 1952, at age fifty-five. Even if Mike had not known his father was alive prior to Effie's passing, he would have become aware in the year of her death. Mike, the oldest son, held control over her remains and possessions. All of the documents I held in my hands as I stood in the master bedroom of the Cherry Hill house were the same documents Mike held in his hands in New York City in 1952.

Mike could have easily visited his father. Jacob was not hiding his whereabouts. There was a photo of Jacob filed within a folder of documents, stamped on the back, "Eagle Fur Shop" with the shop address in Easton, Pennsylvania. The police chief in Easton had written to Effie's lawyer years before her divorce, so she knew Jacob was somewhere in that town. In an application for Social Security,

Jacob identified "Eagle Fur Shop" in Easton as his place of business years after he had left New York City and his family. It seemed he had worked in Easton consistently through the decades.

During my archaeological dig through drawers, I uncovered Christmas cards sent to Mike from Jacob, undated cards with friendly, handwritten notes included. He inquires about Marie, Peter, and Bob, and asks when they are coming to visit. As I stood in what was once Marie and Mike's bedroom incredulously reading the cards aloud to Ellen, I felt a combination of sadness and anger welling within me. I was becoming upset on my father's behalf because he was no longer alive to be upset himself. Mike had kept whatever relationship he had developed with Jacob, for however long that relationship had endured, a secret apart from his brother and the rest of us. The realization that, of course, there was no stranger in a bar who had encountered the name "Stukane" struck like the sudden flash of a strobe light. Effie kept secrets from her youngest son, who believed that his mother was widowed, that he was a fatherless child, and Mike, who knew otherwise, continued his mother's charade.

As I combed through a top drawer in Marie's dresser, I found several notecard-sized envelopes with small photos inside. One envelope held pictures of young Marie and Mike on the beach with friends, Marie's mother, Marie with her sister Olga, and Effie standing next to a man (Jacob?) whose face had been cut out of the picture. In a different envelope, I felt a hard object. This turned out to be a round yellow metal badge with a close-up photo of Effie in the center. It was some sort of work identification: imprinted around the upper edge of the circle: N.Y. Drop Cloth M'F'G. Co., while on the lower rim, under Effie's likeness, the words: Prime Contractor. Like the AM signet ring in a brass Chinese cup, here was another personal artifact of my grandmother parked in an unlikely location.

Effie had been living a lie about her relationship with Jacob, but the few stories my father shared about her industriousness held her core truth. The determined sixteen-year-old who traveled halfway around the world by herself, remained determined. That yellow badge was just the start of my understanding of her drive. More found documents offered insight into her dedication to advancement in her work. A Union Membership Card! My grandmother was in the Bonnaz and Hand Embroiderers, Tuckers, Stitchers, and Pleaters Union, a division of the International Ladies Garment Workers Union (ILGWU).

I unfolded a receipt from the West Side Young Women's Christian Association (YWCA) on 179 West 137th Street in Harlem, where Effie had paid for two 10-month courses on the use of specialty sewing machines: the Zig-Zag and the Mirror. Each course involved fancy-stitch sewing, and I was impressed that when she was fifty-four years old, a year before she died of a sudden heart attack, Effie had decided to learn more sewing machine techniques. (I wondered how well she succeeded in machine-embroidering mirrors on fabric.) I was even more impressed that in order to attend these classes in Harlem, Effie had to undertake lengthy crosstown and uptown subway connections, and do a lot of walking alone. As a New Yorker myself, I knew the time needed, the risks taken, to trek uptown. She had moved close to the Ukrainian community in what is now considered the East Village of Manhattan, so getting crosstown to the West Side and then uptown to Harlem was a significant journey. I liked the determined aspect of Effie's personality, and her commitment to advancing herself. She arrived alone with few or no assets in a country foreign to her, effectively labored using the skills she had, and when she unexpectedly died, she left $11,000 in her bank account, which at the time was a year's middle-class income. I wanted to attach myself to her ambition and detach from her secrecy.

Well into his adulthood, my father thought he had been raised by a widowed mother. He let his older brother handle the paperwork when Effie died and never saw that right there on the death certificate, her status was listed as "divorced." Meanwhile, Mike knew his family story. The documents that told me Effie had requested that the Easton police find Jacob, that she had a warrant issued for Jacob's arrest, that she had successfully divorced Jacob—these were all documents that had been in Mike's possession. In the debris and chaos of the Cherry Hill house, old folders of tattered papers could have easily been fed to a dumpster, but instead, they were now mine to see, touch, and keep. There were certain moments when sorting valuables from garbage in this house of pain and hoarding brought me the pleasure of discovery. Bringing documents of family history to light, I lived one of those moments. I paused to tell the cluttered room that I was grateful to be where I was.

What will always be the greatest mystery for me is why Mike did not confide in Ed, his younger brother, about his relationship with their father when Jacob was still alive. There were notes and greeting cards from Jacob that spoke of visits with Mike and his family, which made me realize that Peter and Bob must have known our grandfather, and they also never said anything to me and my siblings. Mike only chose to tell Ed where their father was living when Jacob was at the end of his life. This was more of Mike's distancing of himself from family. While married to Marie, he found ways to separate himself: he was a traveling salesperson, a Freemason, and a collector of timepieces. I wondered what Mike had told Jacob about Ed. It seemed reasonable to me that as a father, Jacob would have wanted to reconnect with both of his sons. I wondered whether Effie's favorite son might have been Ed, her youngest. Was it possible that Mike could have harbored a resentment that blocked his ability to share? Or was he protecting his "kid brother" from the pain of their parents' separation? That would be the kindest way to view his deception, but hardly in character for Mike.

After all the revelations, I considered whether hidden dramas might exist in every family. Ancestry research is a popular pastime in our current culture, and it often leads to people making surprising, unsettling discoveries. I had thought that my family had no skeletons in any closets. I would have predicted that zero family secrets existed. My experience in the Cherry Hill house overturned my assumptions. I was shocked when I walked into the house of hoarding disorder and saw a situation that I can only describe as surreal. I had never seen so much stuff accumulated in one place before, and saved for decades.

As I delved more deeply into the power and meaning of objects, the house offered greater revelations. Now I had to accept a different, disconcerting family history. Startled by found documents, Effie and Jacob's divorce decree, the warrant for Jacob's arrest, and the awfulness of Mike's deception, I had a new skepticism about what each of us may know about our blood relations, those from prior generations right up until the present. The art of keeping secrets seemed intrinsic to human nature. We just cannot help ourselves, and that fact has been scientifically proven. According to research into secret-keeping led by Dr. Slepian, who is also an associate professor at Columbia Business School, Columbia University, 97 percent of people have at least one long-kept secret at any given moment, and the average number of secrets people hold is thirteen. I had uncovered more secrets than I thought could ever exist in my family.

Effie and Jacob made choices that created a false reality for their son, my father. Growing up fatherless—since he believed what he was told—Ed invented a happy blueprint for what a family should be, and then he created the family he had imagined. I was a child in

Ed's family. His mantra was that we, parents and four children, were crucially important to each other and to the well-being of all of us. Ed succeeded as an adult, to become the father he wanted but never knew, and to make the emotional connections the child in him had needed so badly.

7

Objects Tell Unspoken Stories

In her Netflix stand-up "Have It All," comedian Taylor Tomlinson describes being in the audience of Broadway's "The Music Man" starring Hugh Jackman. As the final curtain descended and the applause settled down, an announcement was made that the Broadway Cares charity was auctioning off a glove Jackman had worn in the play. Being a fan of Hugh Jackman, Taylor wanted the glove that had wrapped itself around the hand of the handsome, talented actor. In her performance, she tells us how she became drawn into a bidding war against another woman who also wanted that glove. The numbers soared. The woman outbid the comedian, but then Jackman appeared onstage and offered the glove from his other hand for Taylor to own. She just had to match the final bid of $7,000. She happily paid the price. This was an object that had touched the body of Hugh Jackman. She describes slipping her hand into the glove and asking it, "What is Hugh Jackman really like?" She opens and closes her fingers in the manner of someone using a hand puppet, and mimics her conversation.

    As I watched Taylor Tomlinson recounting her purchase of Hugh Jackman's glove and how thrilled she felt to be wearing a piece of clothing that had touched him, I realized that her story of connecting with an object was my story too. In my year touching objects in my relatives' home, my understanding of the four people who had lived there, my connection to them, had grown through my contact with their possessions. Their objects held their stories, and sometimes told them in ways I could hear.

Until my year in the Cherry Hill house, I was unaware of the way an object could be a conduit to its owner. Spending such a long time embedded among my relatives' things, I lived through a remarkable, unexpected experience. I came to understand the connective powers of inanimate objects. As I mentioned earlier, my cousin Peter played the accordion and when I tripped over the instrument in his former bedroom, I was brought back to a moment when he lifted it up, took its straps, and placed them on my shoulders. Touching the accordion, I felt Peter's presence and memories of him awakened. Tomlinson's delight in having Hugh Jackman's glove highlighted how possessing an object that someone special once possessed makes you feel closer to that person.

The belief that an inanimate object can carry a history of its owner is an old story. The folkloric search for the Holy Grail comes to mind. This object would just be an old cup no one cared about if the myth that Jesus drank from it at the Last Supper did not exist. Throughout time, people have felt strong connections between themselves and inanimate objects that were once possessed by others. In 1842, Dr. Joseph R. Buchanan, a physician, physiology professor, and eventually dean of the Faculty of the Eclectic Medical Institute in Cincinnati, Ohio, created the term "psychometry," which he described as the ability to divine "emanations" from objects that carried the souls of their owners. Buchanan was a spiritualist who had studied the brain. Today, people who identify as psychics ask to hold objects of people or pets who may be missing. Psychics believe they can figuratively "see" the missing by feeling their energy, their history, through the touch of their possessions. Sometimes, psychics are even sought out by police departments to help solve missing person cases.

The results are mixed, but one case solved with the aid of objects popped up during a CNN interview with Nancy Grace in 2005. Louis Masterbone, a retired detective sergeant in Morris County (New Jersey) Sheriff's Department, spoke of a case in which working with a psychic reunited three children with their mother after thirteen months' separation. The children had been abducted by their father, the mother's ex-spouse, who was under a court order. The mother, who lived in Harding, New Jersey, had suggested that a psychic be consulted. She allowed a chosen psychic to touch and hold her children's toys and clothing. Under the psychic's direction, the police undertook a three-state chase. Masterbone was skeptical at first, but in the interview, he said that the psychic's help had cracked the case and led to the children being found in Hawaii.

I was not eager to enter the world of the paranormal, but I was beginning to feel less dubious about the powerful connections transmitted by objects. After all, I had experienced a strong bond with my grandmother when I had slipped her AM signet ring onto my finger. As I tried to learn more about hoarding disorder, information about the way objects bring their owners into our lives was showing up in my research. In the book *Stuff, Compulsive Hoarding and the Meaning of Things*, coauthor Randy O. Frost, PhD, Harold and Elsa Sipola Israel Professor Emeritus of Psychology at Smith College, wrote in the first person about how he was surprised to learn that students in his seminar highly valued a shirt that had been worn by Jerry Seinfeld, a shirt that a classmate had purchased on eBay. The students told Dr. Frost that "something of the essence of Seinfeld was connected to the shirt," and that this—a hard to describe link—made it particularly prized.

This exchange led Dr. Frost to wonder about a woman whom he was interviewing for his book *Stuff* about her hoarding disorder. What did her possessions give her? He investigated and, as he wrote in the book, concluded that "They connected her to something bigger than herself. They gave her an expanded identity, a more meaningful life. It wasn't the objects themselves that she valued, but the connections they symbolized. . . . We can't help but imagine that some essence of the person or the event symbolized by the objects will magically rub off and become part of us." Dr. Frost then mentions a study that found children valued an object touched by the Queen of England as more important than an identical item the Queen had not touched. Basing an object's value upon who touched it, of course, is the seduction of Hugh Jackman's glove.

However, after making the point about connections in his book, Dr. Frost pondered whether "hoarding has to do not with the desire to be connected to someone or something else, but rather with the fear of being disconnected from a part of oneself." Whether it's a greater connection or a fear of disconnection, the end result is that people bestow upon objects a dynamic and powerful importance. Objects take us to the past while we are in the present. We see in them, and feel in them, the people who touched them. It is this direct connection that breathes life into things that are inanimate.

In the play "I Need That," written by Theresa Rebeck, Sam, an elderly man played by Danny DeVito during the 2023 Broadway run, lives in a house that is packed with significant objects from his life. These items of his past are stacked in piles mixed with trash. Sam, who has a hoarding disorder, is on the verge of being evicted from his home by the local health department. In the course of the play, Sam's daughter Amelia, played by DeVito's real-life daughter Lucy, pushes him to clean out the place. She asks Sam to donate her mother's clothes, which he had draped over the living room sofa, thereby burying the sofa. He sadly talks about how throwing away her clothes feels like saying goodbye to her forever. For Sam, the clothes are not objects separate from his wife. They are her.

How clothing touched by another can come to embody that person, may be in part, because the clothing has a memorable aroma. Anything organic can capture human scent. Each of us sends out our own fragrance. Our bodies are busy combining gland secretions, our body's oils, and its sweat to produce our unique odors. The scent of another is as much woven into the fabric of that person's clothing as the threads themselves are.

My Aunt Marie's clothing was not in the house. Since she had died in 1997 when Mike was still alive, I assumed that he had either donated or discarded her wardrobe. However, items in her dresser, especially her embroidered cotton handkerchiefs, kept her presence in the house. Disposable paper tissues got a big marketing push from the makers of Kleenex in the 1930s, and they eventually replaced ladies' handkerchiefs in American culture. Finding pretty colorful cloth squares in Marie's dresser drawer carried me back to a time when Marie likely used them, in the 1930s, 1940s, and possibly 1950s. Among an assortment, there were two white background handkerchiefs with tiny stars splashed across their surfaces, one with blue stars, one with red stars, each with hand-embroidered edges color-coordinated with the stars. They retained a floral fragrance. For me, this was the scent of Marie. The years had not taken it away. I breathed in the aroma of the blue-starred handkerchief as I brought it close to my face. I could again see my aunt reaching into her beaded purse to find this sweetly scented handkerchief, as she caught a sneeze or wiped her brow.

As I experienced the connection the handkerchiefs created between myself and my aunt, I started to understand more deeply how past possessions could become difficult to throw away. If some aspect of people's beings can be considered comingled within their objects—Jackman's glove, the Queen's cup, my aunt's handkerchiefs—then someone with hoarding disorder surely had to keep those objects around, as they were, in a sense, alive.

Of course, I realized that these connections were not the only motivation for people to accumulate things. The causes of hoarding disorder are vast, diverse, and hard to pin down. Two experts who have researched long and hard to understand why people hoard are Michael A. Tompkins, PhD, and Tamara L. Hartl, PhD. These two clinical psychologists, authors of *Digging Out*, had written in their book that "Sometimes they (hoarding behaviors) accompany other OCD symptoms, but sometimes they don't. More often, hoarding symptoms accompany a wide range of other psychological conditions, including post-traumatic stress disorder (PTSD), bipolar disorder, brain injury, personality disorders, attention deficit/hyperactivity disorder (ADHD), social phobia, eating disorders, severe self-neglect, and Prader-Willi syndrome (a congenital disorder marked by insatiable hunger and developmental delays)." While recognizing all the complexities, I felt that an added motivation to keep objects close was a form of attachment many of us have to the "aliveness" of things. People hold onto items that "speak to them" and offer links to someone or something else.

These emotional links are significant. In *Stuff*, authors Dr. Frost and Gail Steketee, PhD, professor emerita at Boston University School of Social Work, respond to Dr. Frost's students' description of an "essence" of Jerry Seinfeld in his purchased shirt as a "phenomenon." As they comment in their book: "The connection between the object and its former owner transcends rationality. It is symbolic and magical." Frost and Steketee are correct, of course. This connection between an object and its meaning, its aliveness, is not rational, but it remains powerful and shows up in so many ways.

While I was confronting this realization, I noticed how often objects were the topic of conversation in day-to-day life. At lunch together, a girlfriend of mine spontaneously talked about a silver, oval locket she was wearing that had belonged to her mother, and how she felt her mother's presence while she was wearing the necklace. Opening up the locket, she revealed photos of her mother and father that her mother had inserted within the sides of the locket. Her facial features softened as she lovingly gazed at the photos. This object held more than photos. The locket represented the parents my friend loved, who were now deceased.

The exploration of the "aliveness" of an object, the power an object can have, is highlighted in novels, movies, and stories family members pass down through time. It occurs most famously in Marcel Proust's *Remembrance of Things Past*, a novel in seven volumes, with the first volume published in 1913. Proust described drinking tea and biting into a madeleine shell-shaped cake that became his portal to memory and life. The madeleine took the narrator of this novel back in time to his childhood country home and from there into a reflection of the people and places he had encountered. There is a fascination with the hold inanimate objects have on the past. A comfort exists in looking back. Unlike the uncertainty of the present, the past is known.

Centuries may go by, but the drive to understand the relationship between human beings and their objects has no end. In 2013—one hundred years after Proust debuted his opus in 1913—the novel *The Goldfinch* by Donna Tartt was published. An object very different from a madeleine, a painting entitled "The Goldfinch" is the object that drives the action of this book. Theo, the main character, a boy at the start of the novel, steals the painting from a wall of the Metropolitan

Museum of Art in New York. In the book, a terrorist bomb explodes in the museum. Theo's mother is standing in front of "The Goldfinch" painting, gazing at it when the blast kills her. For Theo, the painting becomes his last connection to his mother, and protecting it directs the course of his life.

A main concern for those who love people living with the complexities of hoarding disorder (HD) is that their loved ones are deeply attached not to a few but to *all* of their possessions. Perhaps those who suffer from HD are reluctant to break a bond that began early in their lives. In 1953, the British pediatrician Donald Woods Winnicott wrote that human love for an object can start just after infancy when a child holds tight to a "transitional object." In summary, his finding is: A baby sees the mother as he/she sees him/herself. Baby and mother are one. The mother is an extension of the baby until the baby develops out of infancy and comes to realize that he/she is actually a separate being. This is a shock. Winnicott explains that a "transitional object," a blanket, a doll, or a stuffed animal, is something that a child comes to depend upon for comfort. As a substitute for the mother-child bond, the object can absorb the frightened feelings of a child moving toward independence, and it can offer solace. Often, transitional objects have nicknames and personalities bestowed upon them.

According to Winnicott, an early "transitional object" would be the beginning of a person's relationship with objects, and, as he explains, our first object becomes a stand-in for the mother-child bond. With that primal connection as a basis, it is no wonder that as adults we can feel powerful connections to, and an "aliveness" in, certain objects.

My daughter had a stuffed bunny named Jackson, who now lives in the nursery of her child, my granddaughter. When I lift Jackson up today, I feel that I am holding my daughter's childhood. I have the memory of the mother-child bond from my side, being the mother in the attachment. I may be connected to Jackson as much as, maybe more than, my daughter is. There is an aliveness to the stuffed animal for me. I would never want to see it discarded, and I know from conversations with other parents that I am not alone in this kind of attachment.

Our culture supports stories about the aliveness of toys and approves of special attachments to them. In *The Adventures of Pinocchio*, published in 1883, a wooden marionette becomes a human boy, and more than hundred years later, in 1995 the movie "Toy Story" features action figures, the plastic robot Buzz Lightyear and the wooden cowboy doll Woody, who transform into animated beings that solve problems. The centuries' old concept of aliveness in objects continues. Throughout time, many childhood stories of inanimate objects becoming animate have shaped the perceptions of growing children. With this in mind, when children become adults, why would they not continue to humanize and feel affection for chosen objects?

The comfort that objects create, the presence of another they embody, and the moment in time they hold are reasons we can all recognize for holding onto things, but in the extreme, these reasons become motivations for people to hoard. While I can write about the importance to me of what is primarily a child's toy, I also know that I have given away the majority of my daughter's playthings. I have been able to sort through objects. I feel pain for people who hoard because they have difficulty making decisions and determining what is special. I saw around me in Bob's childhood home, his excessive purchasing of random items like paper towels and blank VHS tapes, as well as his possession of objects that were attached to the lives of his family members. It seemed that every object was equally significant. Yet I still hoped he might have valued more the objects that had been the most personal and with him the longest, like the ten time-worn Chinese Checkers games that were stacked and tied together in the garage. These, I felt, were items more strongly attached to family. Mike, Marie, and their sons, or just Bob and Peter, could have moved their marble pieces many times back and forth across any of the gameboards before me. When he was by himself in this house, which was most of the time, Bob could have relived spirited matches of Chinese Checkers. In my mind's eye I saw him pretending to play a game with his mother or his brother, as he role-played their parts. I assumed that he had saved these games because they were helping him revisit those longed-for, lighthearted moments he once might have shared with people he loved.

I was glad that Marie's extensive collection of what was now vintage jewelry was untouched by Bob and still stored where she had kept it, in the drawers of a small wooden apothecary chest. I opened a drawer and removed from a small plastic bag, first a folded note of description written in Marie's handwriting and then, as Marie's note explained, a necklace of flat white Venetian glass beads, each about one inch in diameter. Dappled red drops mingled with metallic sparkles to define the center of each white bead. I wanted to believe that Bob found solace in touching and holding his mother's jewelry. As soon as I locked the necklace's clasp around my own neck, I mentally slid back in time to the 1940s and my aunt's life. The jewelry instantly connected me to her. I fantasized going out and buying a tailored suit to give the jewelry a proper showing, as Marie might have done. Bob had seen the necklace and many of the other pieces in this jewelry collection on his mother. Marie defined herself by her fashion choices. Mike and then Bob had kept Marie's style safely in place through the decades.

Not far from Marie's apothecary jewelry box, Mike's pipes stood in a circular wooden holder on his dresser. They had been there since he died in 2005. Looking at them, I saw Mike with the black stem of a pipe—it could have been any one of these—between his teeth. One by one, I held each of the six pipes, bowls crafted from varying types of wood. I breathed in the still-lingering aroma of pipe tobacco in each of them. I could smell the fragrance that signaled my uncle's presence in a room. I slipped into a memory of one of the few times I saw my father working with his brother. Mike had come to help my father construct a garage at our home in New Jersey. Above the sound of their hammering, the two of them were shouting instructions loudly to each other on the garage roof. They lifted two-by-fours, dropped them in place, and congratulated themselves. This vision came from the black walnut pipe I had just returned to the holder. I believe it was the one Mike had smoked that day. I sensed it had more stories to tell. My fingers swept across the pipe holder, and I paused. The touch of these objects enveloped me in a strong emotional memory. Could they have created an even more powerful internal response in Bob, who was a core member of the family in this house?

In *So Much Stuff*, author and archaeologist Chip Colwell breaks down humanity's three-million or so years of creating objects, starting from man's first cutting stone and ending with a world that is "overstuffed." In his 10-point listing of our journey to our overstuffed world, his sixth point is this: "The development of symbolic thinking transformed humanity's relationship with things, expanding the possibilities of what things could do for the human imagination and human expression: art, religion, money, gifts, heirlooms, and much more." Objects had at first been created as tools to help humans complete tasks, but they evolved beyond practical purposes. Objects entered the realm of artistry, and once there, they gave rise to emotions.

All of us have attachments to objects that symbolize particular events, that hold the memories, the histories, of cherished people. For those who suffer from hoarding disorder, deciding to let any objects go—to know what to save and what to toss—becomes painful, perhaps even impossible, especially when an object embodies the "essence" of another, someone loved. Comedian Taylor Tomlinson was willing to pay $7000 for the "essence" of Hugh Jackman's glove, and she had never met him. My compassion for my cousin was deepening.

8

What I Did with All That Stuff

Throughout the year, every day I spent in my family-inherited house of hoarding, I stared at those five distinctly labeled boxes: Keep, Auction, Throw Out, Donate, Not Sure. I was choosing how my relatives' possessions would meet their fates. At the end of each day, things in Keep and Auction would be safely stored, Throw Out and Donate were easily dispatched, but the Not Sure pile would always be there, the only one remaining. Objects that held personal memories, that had possible value, that someone else in the family might want or need, were comingled in Not Sure. Family photo albums were definitely Keep. The leaded glass lampshade in the style of Tiffany looked to be a good bet for Auction. What was clearly trash, like a broken garden hose in the kitchen, was a quick Throw Out. Usable dishes were selected for Donate. Deciding what to do with dozens of Not Sure items, however, was exhausting. It was easier to let things like the Lundberg-designed iridescent glass vase, a vintage wooden rocker, and sterling silver salt and pepper shakers sit in Not Sure indefinitely, but I am getting ahead of myself.

In many ways, my experience was similar to the settling of an estate with no will attached. A relative had died, and my siblings and I, being next of kin, had inherited the relative's house. Under normal circumstances, we could have scheduled an estate sale and put the house on the market right away. The difference was the discovery of cramped, unsanitary rooms filled with time-worn contents, the effects of hoarding disorder. An estate sale in a house stacked with piles of possessions, both trash and treasure, where there is little space to walk, is physically impossible. Most likely, my cousin Bob, as the last resident of the house, was the greatest hoarder in the family of four. Following the death of his father, he had lived alone in the house for eleven years, plenty of time to accumulate.

If I had been aware of his hoarding disorder when he was alive, I know I would have tried to help him release himself from at least some of his objects. The amount of stuff, the hundreds—if not thousands—of eclectic objects that Bob left behind, overwhelmed the senses of sight, smell, and touch. To disperse these objects required a cast of many: hoarder housecleaners, auction houses, charities, flea market procurers, real estate agents, and lawyers. Those different piles needed different cast members. (I chose to avoid the time-consuming tasks of listing each individual object for sale on eBay, packing, and shipping them one by one.) Hours bled into days, weeks, and months until almost a full year was devoted to emptying the house, even with helpers on hand.

With Ellen, I cleaned out the oppressive environment of someone who hoards, without the person who accumulated all those objects alive to talk to me about events in his life that might have led him to barricade himself in a fortress of things. Bob was not there to help me make sense of his world. Instead, his things became the clues to who he was, and what happened to them became my story.

Six was the number of days hoarder housecleaners estimated it would take to empty the house. We four siblings were together in the house for interviews with junk removers. At their separately appointed times, two company owners, men about forty years old, arrived to examine the garage, three bedrooms, two bathrooms, attic, basement, and to walk the narrow path between the walls of items piled shoulder-high in the living room, dining room, and kitchen. They each offered a similar plan with similar costs. They had cleaned out houses like ours before. Based upon the square footage of the house, the density of the refuse, and the estimated number of man-hours and dumpsters, quotes ranged from $12,000 to $15,000 for six days of emptying. (Bob's left-behind checking account, now incorporated into an estate account, would cover the fees.)

Sorting was not the job of the cleanout companies; therefore, objects that held the souls and secrets of my uncle, aunt, and cousins, like Mike's smoking pipes and Marie's Murano glass bird, were equal to boxes of batteries and cartons of crackers. We were only a job, a question of numbers to them, but Ellen and I wanted to sort, evaluate, and decide upon the fates of different objects, consigning them to their proper categories. This approach, we knew, would take much longer than six days. One company owner told us that his business's commitments gave him little room to extend his time in the house. Ron Ford, operational manager/co-founder of Hoarders Express (HE), a military veteran with an eighteen-year-old company, agreed to flexibility in scheduling. "Every property is different," Ford told me. "If you just wanted the basement cleaned out for whatever can go into a dumpster, that's just a flat rate, but if we have to sort through things and clean, that changes the whole pricing structure." I knew nothing about hoarding disorder or hiring housecleaners when Ellen and I opened the front door of our cousin's house for the first time.

While HE (recently renamed Hoarders/Clutterers Express) served us well, later, I learned that for far less money than our family paid, I could have personally called a dumpster rental company to drop off a dumpster and pick it up when filled. If you are facing the deconstruction of a cluttered household and want time to make thoughtful decisions, I recommend that you rent a dumpster yourself and if possible, hire workers only—unless you have willing friends—to help sort, organize, and fill those rented thirty-cubic-yard behemoths. You will avoid a deadline and experience huge savings.

We went ahead with our HE partnership and met our helpers on a day in November 2017, after we had removed the vintage Pontiac and Oldsmobile cars from the driveway to make room for the first of six 30-cubic-yard dumpsters. (We were a happy sight for neighbors who came by to introduce themselves, offer assistance, and thank us for uncluttering the property.) Paired with an HE CleanUpper, I began peeling away the outer visible layer of trash in the living/dining rooms and kitchen, all on the first floor. At first, it was easy to identify Throw Out: the dozens of cardboard file transfer boxes, some empty, others filled to capacity, with cleaning supplies, with boxes of unopened plastic storage bags, with outdated computer equipment, with more than one hundred blank VHS tapes. Then, typical of people who hoard because they fear running out of supplies, there were the many tilted piles of packaged toilet paper and paper towels falling onto each other. However, progress slowed when I needed relief from the stagnant, stale odor left behind by the thousands of cigarettes smoked by Mike, Marie, and Bob. The lingering scent of scorched matter in the plaster walls, the smell of tragedy, enveloped me. Breathing became difficult in spite of the mask I was wearing. I frequently escaped to the outside to inhale fresh air.

I also held my breath near the maggot-and-insect-filled refrigerator, and I was especially grateful to the HE workers who carted it away.

They did the same with a six-foot-long horizontal freezer compactly stored with frozen meats, labeled and dated five or more years ago. No question that these big appliances and their contents were in the throw-out pile.

I wondered how the removal would have progressed if Bob had still been alive in this house. Ford explained that when HE is called to clean out a home where a person suffering hoarding disorder is in residence, accumulation has usually reached the point where the state health department has deemed the house unsafe and unfit to live in. If children are residing in the house, the state might be threatening to separate them from their family. "We handle things with kind, compassionate, caring service, but we still get the job done," said Ford. (HE has decluttered homes with hoarded animals, cats, and dogs that had to be rescued, and once discovered a dead cat during a cleanout.)

Ellen and I soon needed more space to sort. Ford offered to bring in a trailer hitched to his truck to provide some additional square footage for $250, a cost we had not anticipated, a fee not addressed as an extra in our signed contract. So instead, we rented a less expensive, more affordable storage unit two miles away, a place where we could relocate, sort Not Sure objects, and store those in Keep and Auction. Decision-making was more manageable at a breathable distance away from the house. This separation caused me to consider that if someone suffering from hoarding disorder is being encouraged to clean out objects, a storage unit may be a gentle way to begin the process.

Working with HE for the year that we did, Ellen and I got to know the cleanout helpers, who consulted with us before discarding items, and Ford was accommodating. Being a local business, he was close enough to check on the house when the ADT security alarm sounded (a scare later blamed on wind and a loose window connection) and the police called Ellen at 10:00 p.m. at her home, more than an hour's drive from Cherry Hill. She contacted Ford, and he represented us on-site, a testament to our trusting business relationship. With a little negotiation, we did use his trailer after all, without a fee, to collect the many appliances and tools found in the house—an electric saw, a vacuum cleaner, drills, and hedge trimmers, among them—for donation to Habitat for Humanity.

I wanted to feel confident about choosing the giveaways for Donate. Sometimes items were difficult to categorize. Should brand-new model trains still in their original packaging be donated, or were they possible moneymakers for the estate that I should hold for Auction? At night, I would go to bed with visions of cut glass bowls, paperweights, Rose Medallion china, and more, moving through my mind like an unstoppable slideshow, while I stood by, a motionless viewer of all that passed before me. Where would my relatives want their possessions to be placed? Did their imagined wishes even matter anymore? I balanced options as I slid into sleep.

An urn with Bob's cremated remains had been settled within a columbarium niche at Grace Episcopal Church in Merchantville, New Jersey. This was my relatives' house of worship. On a lower level, technically called "the undercroft" of the church, a thrift shop was thriving. Suddenly, there was clarity. Here was the logical home for many of their things. After all, Bob currently resided in the church. Ellen and I stacked boxes of commercial Christmas ornaments, and many of Bob's crafts—wires, glitter, beads—for creating his handmade Christmas ornaments, in the back of her Subaru and supplied the Grace Church thrift shop with holiday decorating supplies just before Christmas 2017.

For months we continued to drop off items at the shop, including additional Christmas decorations, a collection of men's flannel shirts from Bob's closet, and Tupperware containers unearthed from Marie's days as a Tupperware Lady selling plastic-covered bowl sets to women invited to home parties. Later on, the women who worked at the shop told us that almost everything we had donated sold out in days.

Occasionally, loaded with usable kitchen dishes, flatware, pots, and DVDs, we would stop at a large Goodwill center along the highway on our end-of-the-day drive back to Ellen's home. Six 30-cubic-yard dumpsters had been filled by the time the house was on the market, even though we had made recycling as many objects as possible a priority. Donating was an avenue to reuse—and donating to a local charity was personally fulfilling. A neighborhood theater company welcomed the usable furniture. However, there was also another, different path for many items, one that could bring money into the estate—the world of auction houses.

When a CleanUpper climbed up the dropped ladder to the attic and passed down what appeared to be a framed drawing he had found at the top step's entry, I had no doubt that the "Auction" category now had a major item. I stared at the artist Robert Rauschenberg's lithograph entitled "Winner" in the frame. Here was collage-style artwork, with images of a long-ago US senator from New York named Jacob Javits imposed over a hazy gray aerial view of New York City. I knew that this Rauschenberg piece, a surprise discovery, should be properly sold. It was time to dive into the internet and test the boundaries of the art world. Research told me that the piece was valuable, probably worth a few thousand dollars.

A representative from Freeman's, an art auction house in nearby Philadelphia, arrived in January 2018 to examine the Rauschenberg. With a portion of the first floor's contents cleared away, when he knocked on the front door, there was just enough room for two people to stand in the entryway. The artwork, propped atop a stack of Model Railroader magazines, caught his attention immediately. He held it close and told me that it was in good condition. He would take it for auction at a future date, and asked whether I had other works of art. Together we traveled the living room path, which wound around the dining room table to Marie's hutch. A Durand vase with signature iridescent gold threads wound around sea-green glass stood center stage on a shelf. He reached in to hold it. Then he noticed a number of carved jade animals—a rabbit, a cat, a bear—and offered to sell all these pieces at auction too. It was agreed that he could take the Rauschenberg lithograph back to Freeman's and Ellen, as administrator of Bob's estate, would travel to Freeman's offices for contract signing. She would also bring along the vase and jade pieces.

Freeman's, the oldest auction house in America, (which in 2023 became Freeman's/Hindman), had a sterling reputation. The pieces we released for auction fit into the Freeman's catalog and reached an audience interested in twentieth-century works of art and upscale items like Chinese jade carvings. The question I faced next was what to do with other items that were not works of art. Things like collected comic books, mantel clocks, and paperweights still held value. Our Freeman's rep became our go-to advisor and recommended Alderfer, an auction house in Pennsylvania that he had worked with and praised as being trustworthy. Personal networking became a powerful, technology-free search engine. Should you find yourself emptying out a home, do ask for recommendations from those you interview at the start, and keep asking. This task needs a lot of helpers.

The Keep pile held fewer and fewer items while "Auction" objects kept accumulating. Whatever did not sell at auction could always be reconsidered for "Keep" or go into "Donate" later on. Then other questions started nagging at me: How do you know that an auction house is accurately pricing your possessions and paying you fairly? Can a commission be negotiated? Are auctions mostly live or online, or both?

By April 2018, six months after we had opened the front door, Ellen and I had slimmed down the contents of the house, so space existed for inviting auction house associates to see what we had to offer. Representatives visited from Alderfer Auction in Pennsylvania as well as an auction house in southern New Jersey. Both offered to send us proposals after seeing everything from the antique telescope in the attic to the ten boxes of marbles in the basement. Since so many of the objects held the energy, the memory of our relatives, Mike, Marie, Peter, and Bob, it became important to me to see how these possessions would be presented and sold to the highest bidder. A road trip to auction locations was in order.

Rain drizzled steadily on the day we drove to the southern New Jersey auction house. Inside the auction building, items were organized in rows of related categories: vintage clothing was grouped in a path that led to handbags, then jewelry, and around a corner, luggage, model airplanes, and on and on the auction displays continued. The surprise was outside, on a grass-patched acre directly behind the building. Rows of objects large and small—appliances, furniture, photographs, jewelry, and more—were spread outside on the ground, unprotected against the rain. The dirt underfoot was quickly becoming mud. Our things could wind up outside in wet weather. After we had worked for months to assure ourselves that nothing of value had been thrown away, I could not bear thinking that those same rescued and cared-for objects would end up drenched and muddy.

What was Alderfer's approach? A sales associate assured us that all of their displays were indoors in their weather-protected galleries. After reviewing the Pennsylvania location, we signed with Alderfer (the auction house receiving a 20 percent commission) and shortly thereafter, its team arrived for a "sort and sift" day. I watched four people enter one room at a time, evaluate, and set certain objects aside. I was pleased to see high interest in Mike's collected clocks and pocket watches, but I felt a twinge when the Russian religious icon paintings, the samovar, and then, the monkey lamp that had been my hallucinatory obsession, were included in the Alderfer Auction pile. These items held heritage and memory. I could relate to someone with hoarding disorder who finds an object removed from his or her world to be deeply disturbing. I found the "sort and sift" day disturbing. Maybe I should keep certain selected objects, not allow them to leave my world. A push/pull sensation seeped through my pores.

The team's chosen items for auction would bring money into the estate, but then I would never see or hold those memory links again. I was blindsided by my own emotional response to saying goodbye to things like the lamp and the samovar. I thought about Bob, who lived among these objects every day, banishing any thought of parting with even one of them. After all, they were touchstones of his life, in effect, tangible and meaningful chapters of his life.

Much as I hesitated, much as I wrestled with inner conflict, I did finally surrender to logical thought rather than sentiment. I let almost all of the selected items leave for auction. Alderfer cataloged every piece and informed us that the vintage toy soldiers would be included in a category auction, under "Antique Toys." Other category groupings, for jewelry, china, and more, would be scheduled for auctions throughout a year's time.

After dumpsters had been filled and removed, auctions scheduled, donations made, keepsakes kept, and undecided items at last decided, the house still had stuff—furniture, odds and ends of china plates and bowls, books, baskets, Peter's hanging wasp nest, all sorts of paraphrenalia. That's when I learned about a cleanout person for the left-behinds. In this last stage of liquidation, a flea market procurer, one recommended by Alderfer Auction, came to the house to do a clean sweep. We paid him a reasonable fee to remove everything.

Presumably, he made future profit by selling things he found in the house. He took away all objects and broom-cleaned each room. Here was a new-to-me specialty occupation. Now the house could be put up for sale, but first I had to catch my breath.

What I learned...

If a loved one with hoarding disorder is ready to organize and do some cleaning out, or if you are emptying a residence where a loved one with hoarding disorder once lived, here is a pathway, a sampling of options for all that stuff:

Hoarder Housecleaners: The twenty-first century has seen an explosion in the waste removal industry in the United States. It is now a multibillion dollar business with 20,000 active companies. The 1-800-Got-Junk internationally franchised company, the largest in the industry, likely brings in $1 billion on its own during a year. From my experience, I found that using the internet for help in choosing a local company with local helpers worked best. It is worth repeating that with his business location in close proximity to the house, Ron Ford, the operational manager at Hoarders Express (HE), www.hoardersexpress.com, was able to represent Ellen and me when the ADT alarm system linked to the local police department was triggered. Trust is a big component of the relationship with housecleaners, auction houses, and later on, real estate agents. Forever decisions are being made with people you have just met.

A personal interview with a housecleaning company is essential for the company, and for you, to have a mutual understanding of the task at hand. Most issues can be negotiated. Again, cost varies depending on the size of the space to be tackled, the density of collected objects, and the sanitary conditions. When someone suffering from hoarding disorder is in residence in a house, caring compassion is needed to remove the fewest items. According to Ford, it is usually a family member or close friend of the person who is hoarding who will contact cleaners.

Hiring a cleanout company that will bring in helpers and dumpsters, which we did, is one-stop shopping. Renting from a dedicated dumpster company that will drop off the dumpster and take it away at an appointed time is more economical. You may be able to hire a cleanout company's helpers only and avoid a higher dumpster price. Much depends on whether a person suffering hoarding disorder is in residence and the agreements that can be reached with that person. Sometimes the sight of a dumpster can be emotionally upsetting. (In Chapter 9, psychologists share the wisdom of their findings about hoarding disorder.)

Professional Organizers: If you are feeling overwhelmed and have the resources to hire a professional organizer for help in deciding what to keep and what to discard, the National Association for Productivity and Organizing Professionals (NAPO) can provide direction through counseling: https://www.napo.net/page/howtohire

Auctioneers: When selecting an auction house, look at its history and reviews, and sign on with the house you trust to treat and market your possessions respectfully. Alderfer Auction met our criteria for honesty and openness. We were always informed about which of their scheduled auctions included our things. After the last sale of my relatives' items occurred, there were surprises high and low. One of Mike's watches, an 1800s silver pocket watch crafted by a well-known nineteenth-century watchmaker, sold for $16,000. However, a colorful Nativity scene by an Italian sculptor who created beautiful 18-inch individual plaster figures of Mary, Joseph, the Wise Men, and also Baby Jesus in a manger, sheep, goats, and a cow, sold for only $1. Apparently, the unexpected is to be expected in the world of auctions.

As John Schultz, president of the National Auction Association, explains: "The industry is made up of thousands of auctioneers who utilize a variety of sales methods, among them, live and online auctions. There's a large group of auctioneers, probably the majority, who have live auctions as a part of their daily auction business and practice." The coronavirus pandemic, however, boosted other options. "Post-pandemic there is definitely a greater percentage of auctioneers who include online bidding in some regard, generally a mix of either online-only options or what are considered simulcast auctions where it's still a live auction but has an online bidding component," says Schultz.

Networking with Freeman's, an art auction house with a reputation I knew, led me to Alderfer auction house, which sent its team to sort and sift and take selected objects to its Pennsylvania location for live auctions.

Due to the unsanitary conditions at the Cherry Hill house, an auction could not take place on the property, but live auctions are often scheduled at estate locations, in homes. "Across the country, live auctions are used for real estate and for items from the most luxurious assets to the least luxurious assets and everything in between," says Schultz.

When I interviewed Grant Souder, sales associate at Alderfer, for any updates, he told me that today, Alderfer auctions are 100 percent online! Also, items are auctioned while still on the premises of the estates involved in the sales. "We still would come out," Souder explained, "but typically we start with some photos (that an individual would send). Based on the photos, we would pair you up with the appropriate sales associate who would come out, do a walk-through and determine appropriate next steps." The sort-and-sift service I experienced, when items are packed up and transported back to the auction center, is undertaken less frequently, according to Souder.

Today that process is used mostly when a home is logistically difficult to access as a site for an estate sale.

To sell through Alderfer Auction, Souder told me, "Oftentimes people will call in and want to talk through the auction process. If that's the case, they can call our main number: 215-393-3000, press 1 for Sales, and they'll likely get me or one of my colleagues. If they prefer to start via email or through the internet, which expedites the process, there's a form on our website." Contact information and up to twenty photos can be uploaded through: https://www.alderferauction.com/buy-or-sell/consign-now. Follow-up steps would include professional photography and cataloging. Online auctions last fourteen days. After objects have sold online, Alderfer picks them up for shipping.

As for other auction houses across the country, after an online auction ends, checkout may take place on-site. A buyer can travel to the house that is the location of the sale and pick up the purchased item right there. Trust, important in creating a relationship with junk removers and house cleaners, is just as crucial with an auction house. You will be selling cared-for possessions and you will want them treated protectively and marketed smartly.

A wise way to begin your selection of a reputable auction house is by contacting the National Auction Association (NAA) online at: https://www.auctioneers.org/. You can choose from among NAA's approximately 3,000 active members by linking to the NAA's "Find An Auctioneer" directory: https://www.auctioneers.org/AF_MemberDirectory.asp. Every member auctioneer meets the NAA's standards for ethics and accountability.

Before you make your final selection, however, interview! If you were looking for an individual agent to sell your house or car, you would ask tough questions to help you choose the person whose abilities you trusted. Your goal is to have that same sense of trust when you partner with an auctioneer. So do not hesitate to ask for references and specifics. Has an auction house had experience with the types of items you are offering? What is the plan for your possessions? John Schultz offers this advice: "Don't be afraid to ask for details, to question and ask for clarifications," and he offers this example: "For instance if I have 500 items in my home or wherever, how are you going to sell them? By 100 lots? 400 lots? One lot and put everything in one big pile? You want to make sure that whatever the strategy is regarding the sale of your items, it makes sense to you. Intuition matters. Just because you're not a professional, you should not discount your intuition and instincts. More often than not, these tend to be correct."

Flea Marketers: The sort-and-sift team at Alderfer recommended the flea market procurer for the final removal of objects left behind in the Cherry Hill house. A local auction house might be a source for finding a flea market procurer, but also, a visit to a flea market may connect you with the right person. Speaking with vendors who may be selling objects similar to the ones you still possess might lead to a more in-depth cleanout. To find flea markets in different states: https://fleamarketzone.com/

Donations: When donating items, local charities felt personally gratifying for me. My relationship with the workers at the Grace Church thrift shop and Ellen's association with a community theater in need of props gave me a chance to know where things, like the vintage rocker, had found new destinies. We also donated to global nonprofit organizations such as Goodwill and Habitat for Humanity, but giving locally was first choice.

Of course, I am writing from my own unexpected life experience. I had to learn along the way who could help me, and how. At the same time, the possessions of my uncle, aunt, and cousins were becoming more personal to me. While making decisions about their objects, sometimes the practical and the emotional rose up together, confusing me as to which was the important course to take. Fortunately, with my sister and I sharing this inherited-house adventure together, I did not have to make decisions alone.

9

When Someone You Love Compulsively Hoards

Whether any family members, friends, neighbors, or coworkers may suffer from Hoarding Disorder (HD) is difficult to know because often it's a painful secret kept behind closed doors—and it can begin to take hold during childhood. During a virtual health conference I attended, a woman working to overcome her hoarding behavior told a personal story. She was in third or fourth grade when, after a guest speaker had finished addressing her class, she approached the woman and asked whether she might have something of hers, like an earring, to remember her visit. Reflecting on her younger self, this woman described how, even then, she was displaying one of the personality traits of HD: worry over memory lapses. People who compulsively hoard are often motivated to possess certain objects because they are concerned that without those objects for visual stimulation, they will forget information, events, and people.

When we were all young cousins together, I had no sign that Bob had hoarding tendencies. As I described earlier, upon entering the Cherry Hill house after he had died, I was instantly shocked, horrified, disgusted, and overwhelmed by the refuse, the smells, the fact that I was connected to this unsanitary situation. I knew Aunt Marie treasured her collected jewelry. Since her gems and perhaps other valuables might be hidden underneath the debris, I soon found myself sorting the possessions of all who had lived there—my uncle, my aunt, and two cousins. After many months, I had learned more about each of them through their objects --their passions, dreams, and disappointments-- than I had ever known. I sensed that for my uncle and aunt, who were collectors, objects became more important than each other, and perhaps even more important than their children.

My initial repulsion slowly and quietly evolved into empathy for Bob. By the time he died, he had become a man living alone in a home that basically stored sorrow. Not one room in the house functioned in a normal way. The living room furniture was buried under, the kitchen stove was coated in layers of grease and dirt, the cabinets were completely blocked, and the one available bed in this three-bedroom house was covered with papers, clothes, leftover soda cans, and rotted food.

How he became a person who accumulated such a hodgepodge will stay buried with him. I recognized the clues, the PTSD, depression, physical pain and reliance on opioids, but a proven link from these issues to his piling up of possessions remained elusive. Perhaps a genetic connection to HD took hold. If I had been aware of Bob's hoarding tendencies when we both were younger, could I have possibly done something to help him create a healthier home environment and bring him out of his apparent isolation? I will never know, but I continue to wonder, "What if?"

It is too late to reach out to Bob, but my guess is that I am likely to meet, or maybe even already know, someone who is accumulating behind closed doors. The International OCD Foundation reports that an estimated 2 to 6 percent of the population lives with hoarding disorder. According to the US Census, the population of the United States was set to reach 335,893,238 million in 2024, which means that the number of citizens with HD has the possibility of ranging from over six million to over twenty million people, and that estimate may be low. Those who hoard are often reclusive and hard to count. During my year in this house where time stood still, I sought an understanding of the roots of hoarding disorder and the ways in which a loved one with HD might be encouraged to seek help, reduce their need to accumulate, and have a more healthful home. Although I cannot help my relatives anymore, perhaps what I have learned can change someone else's life for the better.

I was surprised to discover that most information about HD is relatively new. It was only in the early 1990s that the closed doors of those who were compulsively hoarding began to be pried open with research from Randy O. Frost, PhD, who at the time was a professor of psychology at Smith College, and Rachel Gross. "I really got interested in it (compulsive hoarding) by happenstance," Dr. Frost explained in our interview. (As mentioned earlier, Dr. Frost is currently the Harold and Elsa Sipola Israel Professor Emeritus of Psychology at Smith College, as well as the coauthor of *Stuff, Compulsive Hoarding and the Meaning of Things*.) "Rachel Gross was a student in a seminar I was teaching on Obsessive-Compulsive Disorder. Students had to do a term project on a topic related to research on the subject and she asked me if she could do her term paper on hoarding. It had been mentioned in a few texts."

"I said that it was not a good topic for a research paper because no one sees these patients, it doesn't happen very often, but if she wanted, we could put an ad in the newspaper and see whether we could get someone to interview. She could do a case-based interview sort of study." The local newspaper ad generated 100 phone call responses. As a researcher, Dr. Frost realized that he had encountered a condition people were living with that was related to Obsessive-Compulsive Disorder (OCD), but that this condition—eventually separately recognized as HD—had not been deeply investigated. Dr. Frost went on to become a leader in the study of hoarding disorder after that 1993 research paper he and Rachel Gross authored together: "The Hoarding of Possessions" appeared in the journal *Behaviour Research and Therapy* in May 1993.

Although research by Dr. Frost and his colleagues was bringing more and more knowledge to light about possible causes and treatments, hoarding disorder was considered a symptom of OCD rather than a separate condition until 2013. That's when the American Psychiatric Association, which writes and publishes the *Diagnostic and Statistical Manual of Mental Illnesses* (DSM), made a change. A professional reference book and guide that mental health providers rely on to diagnose their clients, the DSM is a crucial tool of the trade. When the DSM-5 edition was published in 2013, for the first time Hoarding Disorder was recognized as a stand-alone mental health condition in a class of Obsessive-Compulsive Disorders. Now there is much more known about how HD can take hold of a person and cause emotional pain for the individual and for all who hold him or her dear.

As I have mentioned throughout this book, there are no clear-cut causes of hoarding disorder. A significant percentage of people who compulsively hoard also have OCD, but there are many other reasons why people hoard. Researchers suspect that a parent who is emotionally distant may prompt a son or a daughter to fill that deep emotional void with attachments to objects. Genetics may play a part. If others in the family hoard, the risk increases. With a traumatic event that results in Post-Traumatic Stress Disorder (PTSD), the risk increases. Brain and mood disorders such as impulse control, depression, anxiety, attention deficit hyperactivity disorder (ADHD), dementia, all have the possibility of contributing to hoarding, and topping the list of these disorders, studies indicate that over 50 percent of HD sufferers meet the criteria for clinical depression. This can mean that millions of people with HD feel extremely sad, have little energy, low self-esteem, trouble sleeping, barely any appetite for eating, and overall, are disinterested in life and social activities.

Yet those who suffer from hoarding disorder will say they save things for the same reasons we all do. Objects are useful, or sentimental, or appeal to a personal sense of aesthetics. The "saving" just goes to an extreme, beyond clutter, greater than collections. A room can be cluttered with disorganized items, but as long as it still functions, for example, if you can sit on a sofa in a living room, set a cup down on a coffee table, and walk around the space, then the clutter has not become a hoard. Likewise, a collection of themed objects is not a hoard unless the collection disrupts the comfortable use of a room. In fact, a true collector will create a specific place to care for and display artfully selected treasures. My Aunt Marie housed her collection of Asian jade carvings and ceramics in a corner hutch. Another mark of a collector is someone who thoughtfully buys and sells with the aim of reshaping a collection over time. A person who hoards does the opposite, buying impulsively, often in quantity, without thought as to where purchased items will go.

Now there is a difference between hoarding behavior and hoarding disorder, which Gail Steketee, PhD, professor emerita and former dean at Boston University's School of Social Work, described to me: "Hoarding behavior is just a term for people who save too many things, who acquire too many things and have difficulty letting go of them, that's hoarding behavior in a nutshell, from mild to severe. Hoarding disorder crosses the line. The behaviors that I just mentioned actually interfere with people's functioning, and they too can be mild, moderate, and severe." Dr. Steketee has been researching hoarding disorder for decades. She is coauthor with Dr. Frost of *Stuff, Compulsive Hoarding and the Meaning of Things*, the previously mentioned breakthrough book that shares true stories of people with HD. Her latest book, *Hoarding, What Everyone Needs to Know*, written with coauthor Christiana Bratiotis, PhD, MSW, associate professor at the University of British Columbia School of Social Work, gathers between its covers the last twenty-five years of research into hoarding disorder. Dr. Steketee explained that when hoarding disorder causes distress, "The distress isn't always to the person who is hoarding, although inevitably they are distressed in some way, but often the people around them are quite distressed."

When someone you love is compulsively hoarding, it is normal to feel concern, anger, and a degree of hopelessness. As your loved one continues to hoard items that seem to make no sense or have little value, your distress level can rocket. You would like to rescue your family member or friend from the clutter, helping them to turn the rooms in their homes into comfortable, airy spaces that fulfill their design functions. Yet your loved one repeatedly refuses to throw out items that could make his or her home more livable and sanitary. This is where fortitude is needed on your part. It will take a long time to make any significant changes in a home where someone is suffering from hoarding disorder, but inroads can be made with patience and understanding. Before approaching a loved one who suffers from HD, it helps to understand what thought processes may be at work.

Many of those who suffer from HD have experienced a traumatic event or events in their lives. My cousin Bob, whom I believe suffered HD, was assaulted by a man who pistol-whipped him in his thirties, and when he was in his forties, he faced the deaths of his brother from HIV-AIDs, his mother six months later, and a few years after that, a car crash left him with an inoperable back injury and relentless pain. He became unable to work and lived his final years in thrall to OxyContin. Events surely differ, but often HD sufferers are survivors of past traumas. The accumulation of objects, the saving of stuff, which manifests as hoarding, becomes their method of survival, a way to live with purpose. This lifestyle is isolating, unsanitary, and a contributor to depression.

While anger and frustration are logical reactions when you realize that someone close to you is compulsively hoarding, kindness and understanding are needed. For example, your brother may feel that you, as a sibling, are ready to judge him harshly, and if he views you as angry or frustrated by his choices, he could shut you out. You will want to keep avenues of communication open. Building trust through empathy is a slow process but worth the effort if your brother eventually believes you understand him. Then, with care, you have a chance to talk to him about shedding some of his things.

Although it is difficult to understand why someone compulsively hoards to the detriment of family, career, and social life, certain personality traits are common to this behavior. These traits, actually aspects of behavior, were outlined in 1996 in what has come to be called a "seminal paper" about hoarding disorder. Published in the journal *Behaviour Research and Therapy*, "A Cognitive-Behavioral Model of Compulsive Hoarding" by Randy O. Frost and Tamara L. Hartl, was written when both were in the Department of Psychology at Smith College. Their early attempt to delve into the behavioral roots of hoarding resulted in findings that continue to ring true today. The person you love who is hoarding may have a few or most of the traits described by the authors, but knowing the existence of these mental health situations may offer you that "Aha Moment," that personal epiphany: *Yes, this is a reason why he may be hoarding.*

Frost and Hartl highlight four important psychological categories—**Information-Processing Deficits, Emotional Attachment, Behavioral Avoidance, Beliefs About the Nature of Possessions**—that influence compulsive hoarding actions. By naming these categories, the researchers created helpful labels for understanding how the mind of someone who hoards may work. Below, I have summarized their findings:

1—Information-Processing Deficits

For those with HD, the thought-processing deficits the authors describe are in three areas of what today might be called "executive functioning." They list these areas of deficiency under the following headings:

Decision-Making, Categorizing and Organizing, Difficulties with Memory

A deficit in **Decision-Making** can arise because someone who hoards does not want to make a mistake. What to do? Perhaps a future use for an object will occur, so it ought to be saved. Also, a concern that an object might not be attainable in the future could lead someone to keep it around. The item may be irreplaceable. Compounding these feelings, the researchers reported that merely seeing a possession can increase a hoarder's need to keep it rather than throw it away.

Categorizing and Organizing is another difficulty for many of those with HD because they have an underlying belief that each possession has its own uniqueness. If an object is truly one-of-a-kind, it cannot be categorized or organized into a place where similar objects might go. There are no similar objects! Frost and Hartl describe how someone with HD can pick up an object, and then, not knowing what to do with it, set it down. They watched this happen over and over with different items until many piles accumulated. They named this behavior "churning."

Perceived **Difficulties with Memory** occur among those with HD because they believe that an abundance of information—much more than a non-hoarder would consider—should be retained. Physical items are saved so they will not be forgotten. Frost and Hartl write about how one of their clients kept old newspapers because she feared that she would not remember the information in them. And because those who hoard rely on what they see to help them remember, piles form.

2—Emotional Attachment

We all have objects that we keep for sentimental reasons such as souvenirs from trips taken, jewelry worn by grandparents, or childhood toys, but for those who hoard, possessions can go beyond being nostalgic reminders that could be placed on shelves. People with HD can easily regard their possessions as extensions of themselves, and they do not want those possessions touched or moved. Possessions can also provide comfort and emotional security to those who hoard during anxious moments.

3—Behavioral Avoidance

As Frost and Hartl report, this trait is related to the already-mentioned inability to make decisions for fear of making mistakes and not being perfect. What happens when someone avoids a decision that might have resulted in an object being discarded is that the still-possessed object just gets set aside in a pile. Another reason a person hoarding may avoid change is the fear of loss, of never again seeing an object that offered comfort or some other emotional benefit. The problem here is that for someone who compulsively hoards, many objects may offer emotional attachment. I found avoidance of another kind, though, on the dining room table of the Cherry Hill house, where a mountain of unopened mail, ten years' worth of unopened mail, teetered precariously. Bob clearly avoided opening any envelopes that may have asked for follow-up decisions from him. The mail-made mountain just kept growing, a physical reminder of his delay in decision-making.

4—Beliefs about the Nature of Possessions

To help a loved one change the pattern of hoarding, you really have to understand the deep connection that your person has to his or her possessions. Frost and Hartl discovered that people who hoard want to control the objects they own. If someone else touches or moves them, they may no longer offer safe refuge. Along with this need to control is a belief that objects ought to be cared for and kept because they may have future uses. There is a drive to protect possessions, to keep them safe from harm. Perhaps, for hoarders, protecting possessions is akin to keeping themselves personally safe.

Frost and Hartl's 1996 analysis of the thoughts and perceptions of those with HD can offer you insights into how your loved one might be thinking and feeling. The personal stories told by HD sufferers in *Stuff* by Frost and Steketee also offer an appreciation of how those who hoard look at life. Marnie Cooper, an acting coach whose Facebook page is "A Hoarder Comes Clean," revealed this: "The big question is: Do I love my stuff more than my family, and that's a killer question. The truth is absolutely not!!! And I have a disorder. Both are true. It's hard to explain to family members that I love them more and I can't let go of this salt shaker."

The person you care about with HD places emotional value on his or her possessions, and if you want to connect with your loved one in order to help him or her create a clutter-free space, your respect for those possessions is crucial. A trusting, respectful relationship will be the foundation upon which change can come. However, that change, which may only be incremental, will take patience, and there will be relapses along the way.

Most people with HD do not reach out to therapists on their own for help. Some are not even aware that they need help. Yet, being a family member or a friend of long-standing, you probably remember that their home functioned normally at one time, before piles of stuff were stacked in rooms. You may be able to jog your loved one's memory about how objects piled up over time by sharing the Clutter Image Rating (CIR), a free cellphone app created by Boston University that offers visual views of what happens inside a home when objects keep accumulating: https://apps.apple.com/us/app/clutter-image-rating/id981642952. Nine photos taken in each of three rooms in a home: kitchen, living room, and bedroom, show the progression of stuff and the buildup of items in each room. The photos are rated from 1 (no clutter) to 9 (severe clutter). The CIR is a helpful tool designed to encourage awareness of what's happening in a home. Ask your loved one to compare the living room in his or her home with the living room photo it most resembles in the CIR app. A rating will appear alongside the selected photo. The rating of 4 or above means that a room has too many things within its walls. In a calm, caring manner, you can question your family member or friend about how he or she feels when looking at the photos. At its most successful, the CIR can offer perspective and stir privately held emotions.

With empathy and understanding, you can begin to ask your loved one about his or her dreams. How would your dear friend or family member like to be living? Where would he or she want to be right now as compared to where they are? This nonjudgmental approach is a type of **Motivational Interviewing,** a professional technique that trained therapists use to nudge clients who are resistant to, or ambivalent about, change. Would your loved one be willing to visit with a therapist who practices this technique? Or allow a therapist to visit his or her home to talk? If the answers are "Yes," you are fortunate. Since resistance to therapy is more common than openness to therapy among those with HD, you may want to consult a therapist yourself for the best way to speak with your loved one. With lessons from a therapist, you may be able to acquire motivational interviewing skills, and become familiar with asking open-ended questions and affirming your loved one's abilities and emotions. This technique also trains you to become a patient listener. You will be building mutual trust, removing shame and blame. Slowly, hopefully, you can influence your loved one to consider change, to accept help.

For a greater understanding of motivational interviewing: https://positivepsychology.com/motivational-interviewing/

Harm Reduction

When you have a confident conversational approach in mind and decide to start speaking with your loved one about changing their home environment, you may face resistance or refusal to change. Suggestions for moving forward if your loved one is **open to change** are offered later on in this chapter. For making inroads with someone who may be **reluctant to organize** or discard items, an approach called **Harm Reduction** focuses on making your loved one's home safer. Harm Reduction originated decades ago. One example is the clean needle exchange program, which allows drug addicts to exchange used needles for sterile ones at approved centers as a way to reduce the high risk of exposure to HIV from shared needles. The clean needle exchange does not overtly combat drug addiction but rather, it aims to reduce the spread of a dangerous virus. In a similar fashion, harm reduction for HD does not overtly confront hoarding behavior but instead, focuses on bringing safety measures into an unsafe environment. Michael A. Tompkins, PhD, psychologist and codirector of the San Francisco Bay Area Center for Cognitive Therapy, evolved and adapted harm reduction for HD, and he explains how it works in his book *Digging Out*, coauthored with Tamara Hartl, PhD, psychologist at Pacific Anxiety Group.

Your conversational approach, how you talk to your loved one, is most important. Whatever you can do to build a positive relationship will benefit both of you. Over time, as a loved one continues to accumulate objects, relationships can become distressed, with arguments and pushback, resentment and hurt feelings, and the acceptance of help is shut down. Forgiveness is emphasized for harm reduction. Time and patience are needed for your mutual trust to grow.

Once you have your relationship on a solid footing, you can introduce aspects of the Harm Reduction approach. Hoarded objects create obstacles that block spaces needed for cooking, cleaning, sleeping, and generally moving through a home. The situation can become dangerous to the health of a person with HD, by putting him or her at risk from fire, falling, and other problems, like mold, dust, vermin, which appear in unsanitary environments. In *Digging Out*, Drs. Tompkins and Hartl explain how to undertake a **Home Assessment**, with your loved one understanding that your goal is to make his or her home safe. To calm your loved one, remind him or her that your goal is safety and comfort, not a clean out. The authors recommend that another family member join you (with your loved one's permission) as you identify targets that present safety hazards. Staircases, the kitchen stove, bathroom sinks and toilets, blocked exits, and overburdened electrical sockets are all potential dangers. For example, a stovetop that is still being used for cooking would be a target, especially if there are papers and other flammable items nearby. For each target, you will be working with your loved one to make the space safe. In doing so, you will be encouraging him or her to move, discard, or organize objects in a new way, with an understanding of the need for safety.

A Harm Reduction Plan asks for a "contract" signed by you—and anyone else who may be involved in helping you—and by your loved one. A contract can be a way to calm a loved one's apprehension about accepting help. It can state when your loved one will allow you and possibly others to assist in home visits. It can list the harm reduction targets clearly. A commitment to keep targets risk-free in the future can be in the contract too. Of course, the contract should also be flexible in terms of a time goal. In addition to family members, friends, or close neighbors, a team might also include professionals such as a professional organizer, a handyman for repairs, and a home healthcare professional who can recommend how to handle medications.

People with HD are likely to be more open to a Harm Reduction approach than agreeing to the alternative of strangers coming into their environments and attempting to remove their possessions. They also want to feel in control of their spaces. As Dr. Tompkins explained to me when we spoke for this book: "If someone with hoarding disorder isn't open to help or treatment and you want to help, Harm Reduction is an approach. Using this approach doesn't necessarily mean that it's going to work, but it's not going to make it (hoarding) worse." He was almost poetic when he described the ambivalence of those who have hoarding disorder as they struggle with behavioral change: "When 'No' is the response, the first goal is to move people from 'No' to 'Maybe.' Then they are in 'Maybe' a little while but they slip back into 'No.' It's back and forth between 'No' and 'Maybe.' After working with them, maybe they might spend a little time in 'Yes' but then they go back to 'Maybe.' Then they go back to 'No.' In five minutes a person might go through all those options." Changing a behavior takes time. How many of us have said that we're going to exercise more but procrastinate when the time comes to head out for the gym?

Helping a loved one with HD to alter his or her habits is an undertaking that works when you have patience, education from books like *Stuff* and *Digging Out*, and a good relationship between you and your loved one. In my conversation with Dr. Tompkins, he emphasized the fact that a loved one's motivation is influenced by the quality of interpersonal relationships. His advice:

> Motivation for a loved one to accept your help starts with improving your relationship with that person. If the relationship is very very distressed then their motivation to accept your help will be very very low, so the place to start is by healing those wounds, engaging in conversations that are meaningful, caring, and thoughtful. Let go of trying to fix, trying to focus on, stuff. Focus on your relationship because that's the path, the first step in actually helping a person with a hoarding problem.

To understand HD more deeply, its causes, symptoms, and available treatments for your loved one, psychologists interviewed for this book strongly recommend the International OCD Foundation's links:
https://hoarding.iocdf.org/for-families/
https://hoarding.iocdf.org/for-families/how-to-help-a-loved-one-with-hd/

https://hoarding.iocdf.org/about-hoarding/how-is-hoarding-disorder-treated/

Note: You, as a family member distressed over a loved one's hoarding, may find Family-As-Motivators (FAM) training a good fit. In a 2014 study led by Gregory S. Chasson, PhD, psychologist, associate professor, and director, Behavioral Interventions of the Obsessive-Compulsive and Related Disorders Clinic, University of Chicago, FAM was introduced as a pilot program. FAM's manual teaches therapists how to train family members—first, to cope with a loved one who suffers from hoarding disorder, and second, to motivate him or her to consider therapeutic help. Aspects of Motivational Interviewing and Harm Reduction are folded into the training. FAM consists of 10 one-hour sessions.

An online slideshow from Dr. Chasson explains Family-As-Motivators: https://www.slideshare.net/slideshow/gregory-chasson-family-support-and-intervention-for-hoarding/64484643

For a fee, Copper Bridge Counseling offers Family-As-Motivators webinars: https://www.copperbridgecounseling.com/product/build-curious-compassion-for-the-one-who-hoards/

Cognitive Behavioral Therapy, One-to-One or in a Group

Not all HD sufferers are resistant to help, however, and if a loved one shows signs of wanting to change behavior, you can encourage him or her to seek therapy treatment. In fact, a person who hoards may have quietly tried to reorganize his or her home, may have made attempts to move objects around, but then given up. A cycle of trying and failing can increase a feeling of hopelessness. Efforts a person makes to change circumstances may also be hindered by other issues of mental health such as OCD, depression, anxiety, PTSD, impulse control, ADHD, and possibly dementia. If your loved one acknowledges a degree of hoarding behavior and shows any openness to behavioral change, you have an opportunity to reach out with empathy and support. Your family member or friend may be able to understand the force that is motivating him or her to hoard by entering into Cognitive Behavioral Therapy (CBT) either directly with a therapist or in a group setting. For one-to-one help, you can begin to search for a therapist who specializes in CBT through the International OCD Foundation (IOCDF) which offers help for hoarding disorder on its website: iocdf.org

At its core, CBT is talk therapy that helps people reflect upon how they think (the cognitive part) and act (the behavioral). Drs. Frost and Steketee designed and tested a form of CBT specifically for treating hoarding disorder, and their approach is widely used by therapists today. The best way to describe CBT for hoarding is to quote Drs. Steketee and Bratiotis' book *Hoarding*. The authors write that the treatment "includes education about hoarding and acquiring, goal setting and techniques to enhance motivation for treatment, skills training for organizing and decision making, practice resisting urges to acquire, practice sorting and discarding objects." The therapy also helps people who are hoarding to evaluate the beliefs they hold about possessions. A CBT therapist will want an HD sufferer to talk as deeply as possible about how he or she sees the world and their place in it.

While no drugs have been specifically designed for treating HD, a group of antidepressant medications called selective serotonin reuptake inhibitors (SSRIs) have been recommended for HD sufferers. SSRIs are prescribed by therapists for mental health issues such as depression, anxiety, PTSD, and OCD. People with those conditions are often living with hoarding disorder as well. The medication allows serotonin, which is a mood regulator, to remain at increased levels in one's body. Technically, serotonin is a neurotransmitter that sends chemical messages from nerve cells in the brain to the pathways of the central nervous system and throughout the body, where it influences happiness, memory, hunger, sleep, and sex drive. A lack of serotonin is believed to contribute to depression, anxiety, and so on.

Research results have shown that while the medications helped to ease OCD symptoms, they offered little relief for HD. Randomized controlled studies focusing on the effectiveness of these medications on hoarding disorder alone are needed, but meanwhile, SSRIs continue to be prescribed. Therapists evaluate the full range of issues facing their clients who have HD and make decisions about whether particular drugs may be helpful.

During CBT treatment, therapist visits to the home offer greater tools of understanding for the therapist to use when counseling your loved one. In 2007, Drs. Frost and Steketee wrote *Treatment for Hoarding Disorder* (2nd edition published in 2014), a professional manual for CBT therapists to use when treating individuals with HD. Studies show that the best results come from therapy lasting twenty-six weeks, over the course of six to nine months. The longer the commitment, the better the chance that change will last, as your loved one gradually begins to clear clutter. Your loved one will need your patience and long-term understanding. By the end of the twenty-six weeks, you ought to see more air and space in the house, but it is not likely that all the clutter will be gone. Change comes slowly. (Health insurance may cover the cost of sessions with a cognitive-behavioral therapist. Without insurance, a fifty-minute session can range from $60 to $250 depending upon the therapist and where he or she is located.) A 2021 analysis of the results of twelve studies of CBT for HD reveals a 35 percent clinically significant change overall in HD severity. That is not a high percentage, but it is promising. Until Drs.

Frost and Steketee wrote their therapists' manual describing CBT for treating hoarding disorder, there was no clearly recognized way to help those with HD.

Today, people who hoard can consult a CBT-trained therapist for individual help with HD, but another option is group therapy. After Drs. Frost and Steketee wrote their manual for professionals, there were still relatively few therapists treating HD, so they took their knowledge and created a self-help book. Authors Drs. David F. Tolin, PhD, psychologist, founder and director of the Anxiety Disorders Center at the Institute for Living, Frost, and Steketee, crafted *Buried in Treasures, Help for Compulsive Acquiring, Saving, and Hoarding*. The book, now in its second edition, is informational, but mostly it is a workbook that asks readers with HD to answer pages of questions that aim to reveal the intimate underpinnings of their hoarding. Questionnaires delve into personal values and goals, as well as one's motivation for acquiring, strategies for sorting and removing, and more. The workbook has given rise to workshops that offer group therapy sessions led by either a therapist, a social worker, or a peer who has managed to control HD.

Buried in Treasures workshops, based on the workbook, have formed both online and face-to-face across the country, usually under the umbrella of social services organizations. These can be free or may require a payment, depending upon the workshop, and the number of sessions. Buried in Treasures workshops generally meet for weekly two-hour sessions over twelve to sixteen weeks. (Internet research should help you find a workshop near you. A Zoom workshop from The Organizer Coach https://theorganizercoach.com/buried-in-treasures has an early registration fee of $600, with a regular fee of $650.) The workshops are shorter in duration than the twenty-six weeks recommended for individual therapy, but as noted in *Hoarding*, they have reduced hoarding symptoms by about 24 percent for those who have attended. **These workshops, it is important to remember, are not for family or friends, but for the person who is living with HD.** For those who believe their hoarding issues are not severe enough to warrant individual therapy, the workshop setting is sometimes easier to accept. In a workshop, people with HD open up to peers who live in similar home environments. Encouraging a loved one to explore a Buried in Treasures group workshop might lead to him or her revealing to peers, personal triggers for hoarding. The workshop aims to nudge someone with HD toward a reduction in clutter, while bringing greater awareness to personal hoarding behavior.

A new angle was added to the Buried in Treasures workshop when, in 2023, researchers at Stanford Medicine combined it with Virtual Reality. Nine people over age fifty-five in a workshop were asked to take photos and videos of their most cluttered room, along with thirty other possessions. The photos and videos were changed into a 3D Virtual Reality. For one hour during weeks seven to fourteen of a Buried in Treasures workshop, each person was able to virtually experience recycling, donating, or trashing their objects, which were removed in a virtual trash truck. The participants in the study were then asked to discard the actual objects. Seven of the nine HD sufferers were able to reduce their hoarding symptoms by about 25 percent, which is about the same reduction that happens for those participating in a Buried in Treasures workshop alone. However, researchers see Virtual Reality as a possible adjunct to therapy in the future.

A search on the internet for "Buried in Treasures workshop near me" hopefully will lead you to a group workshop in your area.

Background information on the Buried in Treasures workshop can be found on the site of Mutual Support Consulting LLC: https://www.mutual-support.com/the_buried_in_treasures_workshop

The International OCD Foundation also has a "Hoarding Disorder and Buried in Treasures Support Group" on Facebook to help your loved one: https://www.facebook.com/groups/2173610616110515

Often, it is a family member who is contacted when a hoarding situation becomes apparent to neighbors. It might be debris piling up on the front porch and lawn of a home or odors from an apartment that become alarming to others. Before a notice from a town health department or an eviction from a landlord, coop, or condo board arrives, and while time is on your side, you might consider the options introduced in this chapter.

By now you are probably aware of the deeply emotional connection your loved one has with his or her possessions. HD may also exist alongside other mental health issues. You have a delicate task when, with empathy, you decide to cajole someone you love into accepting help. Nothing will happen quickly.

I am reminded of a tragedy, improbable but true, that ensued in a family where three siblings failed to recognize the attachments their brother had to his hoarded objects. The 59-year-old brother, an auto mechanic, had been living with his mother. When she died at age ninety-five, his three siblings wanted to sell her house quickly. They did not consider how frightened and panicked the brother would be to have his home and his many, many gathered possessions removed practically overnight. When the three siblings and a niece visited their brother at the house to plan the sale, he shot and killed them all with a rifle and then killed himself. This horrific, extreme, mentally imbalanced reaction by the brother was shocking to hear when it was reported on local news programs.

Afterward, I thought about the deep fear of loss that can plague a person living with a hoarding disorder, someone who wants to hold on to as much as possible. The depth of someone's emotional attachment to objects cannot be underestimated. Empathy, gentleness, and patience are crucial to your connection with your loved one. A sympathetic relationship offers a foundation for trust. You have a chance to influence change in your loved one when mutual trust and genuine caring concern for each other are never in doubt.

Epilogue
Closing the Door and Burying Bob

A year after Ellen and I had unlocked the front door of our relatives' home, we turned the same key in the same lock and opened that same door, but this time we entered empty airy rooms that echoed to the sound of our voices. The house was a shell. A few pieces in the living room—a lamp, two chairs, and a small round table next to the entry—were left for a real estate agent to use when showing the house. Why didn't I feel the elation I had expected to feel from a job well done? Oh, I was happy to breathe the air that had been cleansed of musty smoke and burning odors after the dumpsters were filled, but like a cloud blocking the sun, a sadness tempered what should have been a joyful sense of accomplishment for me. As the number of objects that I could match to either Mike, Marie, Peter, or Bob, increased my understanding of each of them, I realized that their stories were affecting my own. Mike's timepieces, Marie's Tupperware, Bob's paintings, Peter's musical instruments—all held within them dreams of who each of them could be. I had witnessed the beginnings and endings of those dreams.

Today I sometimes stare at my own possessions with my year's long, hard-earned knowledge and realize that they tell my story, my starts and stops. The books about calligraphy, the sets of pens, the bottles of ink I purchased to help me develop a new skill, all these objects have become dusty reminders of a challenge never met. The DayGlo mini-dress from my discotheque dancing days will never fit me the way it used to, but still, I keep it in my closet. Our objects are pieces of our lives, our tangible autobiographies.

After my first sight of the hoarded possessions in my relatives' home, family ties began to tug. Even in the mess, I recognized a lamp, a clock, and a few other pieces. I knew I would not do a wholesale dumping of everything, but I would take the time to treat each object that was not obvious trash with respect. I would find the meaning behind each item. By taking this approach, I turned myself into a detective, and soon objects revealed the inner lives of my family members to me, along with family secrets. I also recognized the house itself as an object, one that held the energies of those who had lived there. My motivation, to act with thoughtfulness and care, led to unexpected revelations and an insight into hoarding disorder, a condition I learned more and more about as my year in the house progressed.

For the way I remembered my relatives' early pride about their home and neighborhood, for my own genetic connection to each of them, and for my year of intimacy with them through their objects, for all these reasons, and also for the karmic respect I hoped others would give to my life's possessions, I wanted the house to be presentable. Not everything needed to be repaired, but I thought enough breaks and holes could be mended to change the environment from squalid to merely rundown.

The house gutters looked like meadows with thick vegetation, and Morning Glory vines trailed down from their gutter perches to the dirt below. The backyard resembled a vacant lot, covered with spindly switch grasses that were so dense I could not forge a path. I thought about how ironic it was that Mike's money would pay for anyone

Ellen and I might hire to repair or improve the property that he and his family had allowed to visibly age. Mike had been so reluctant to connect with his brother and his brother's family—my family—and from what the house revealed, even reluctant to connect deeply with his wife and sons. Yet here I was, an inheritor (with my siblings) of his invested money and a caretaker of his life's possessions. He had kept his distance, held his feelings close, behaved as if he were an only child, and now here we were, his brother's children, people he never attempted to know, owning everything he had squirreled away in the course of his life.

I knew that the house was going to survive its inhabitants. It had been neglected but not destroyed. For the final time, I closed the front door I had entered a year earlier and felt that I was done but not quite finished. One important object, a last item on a long list, needed attention: What to do with Bob's cremated remains!

Bob's ashes had been placed within a columbarium, a wall niche for funeral urns located within the Grace Episcopal Church in Merchantville, New Jersey, where Mike, Marie, Peter, and Bob had worshiped during their lifetimes. However, more than a church, it was a community and family. Earlier I had written that Father Jeffrey Kirk, pastor of the church at the time, had talked about presiding over Bob's funeral service at the church and giving Bob's cremated remains a home there, since everyone in the church community believed he had no family. In speaking with Father Kirk again, I realized that his involvement with Bob was greater than I had thought.

I had been living with the assumption that Bob's friend Ted had discovered Bob's deceased body on the floor within the house's entryway when he returned from Christmas holidays with his family. Ted, who had become somewhat of a caregiver for Bob, had told me that he felt guilty about leaving him alone for several days, and he became fearful when Bob did not answer his cellphone. My understanding from Ted was that he had visited the house, discovered Bob, and called the local police.

Father Kirk remembered the day Bob's body was found differently because he had been called to help. It was Father Kirk who had contacted the Cherry Hill Police Department and was present at the house when the police removed Bob's body and crisscrossed the yellow "POLICE DO NOT CROSS" tape across the front door. Father Kirk had been notified, not by Ted, but by a woman I will call Linda, who was a friend of Bob's and Ted's, and she also knew Father Kirk. I had spent a year trying to solve the mysteries of the house and the people in it, and as I was nearing the end of my time in Cherry Hill, moving toward the conclusion, I had to reconfigure the start. It turned out that the early information I was given by Ted was not as accurate as I had believed. There were a few plot twists. I wrote and called Linda to learn anything she would like to share with me about Bob and the day everyone learned he had died. She did not respond. I now understood that it was Father Kirk who had watched over Bob's last exit from the house. It was also Father Kirk who gave Bob's ashes a resting place in the church. When Ellen and I opened the door that brought us more intimately into Bob's life, we were both horrified and surprised. Now, when we were closing the door, having learned more about his life, we uncovered new facts about his death.

Ellen and I did not like leaving Bob's remains alone in a columbarium. He was by himself when he died and was clearly isolated in his final years, but he need not be left alone in whatever may be the afterlife. We would bury him with his parents. When asked, Father Kirk agreed to conduct a brief ceremony at the gravesite, wherever that might be. We knew where to go.

Most of our family history from my father, Ed, and his brother Mike was anchored in the brothers identifying themselves as Russian. When Mike married Marie, another first-generation American born of Russian immigrants, the two remained closely connected to Russian culture, spoke to each other in Russian, and socialized with other Russians at a resort called Rova Farms, in Jackson Township, New Jersey, barely an hour's drive northeast of Cherry Hill.

Rova Farms was an idyllic lakeside retreat of 1,400 acres developed in the 1930s by and for Russians who fled the Soviet Union. It was not unlike the bungalow colonies in New York's Catskill Mountains that became vacation escapes for Jewish families after the Second World War. Newly arrived Russians had an "anti-communist" place to vacation with each other, share their culture, and send their children to socialize together in a Russian camp. Acreage was set aside for cooperative farms that cultivated vegetables favored in Russian cuisine, like carrots, potatoes, cabbage, and onions. Photos pasted into old albums I rescued from a box in the house pictured Mike and Marie by the lake at Rova Farms, only a short walk from where they would be buried, up the hill at St. Vladimir's Memorial Cemetery.

Although I had never visited St. Vladimir's Cemetery, my brother Ed (named after my father) had accompanied our mother to Marie's funeral and burial at St. Vladimir's. He had spoken about the graveyard adjacent to the golden-domed St. Mary's Russian Orthodox Church. Again and again, the thought kept crossing my mind: the world of our objects, to a significant extent, defines us all. The headstones in a cemetery, the gold symbols in places of worship, the urn with Bob's ashes—all were objects of tradition and culture. I had been deciding what to do with so many nontraditional items during the last year, but for this final object, Bob's remains, the choice was clear.

The day was overcast and cool, a fall-like day even though it was summer when we four siblings gathered at St. Vladimir's with Father Kirk, who arrived with his wife. He held in his hands the boxed urn with Bob's remains and The Book of Common Prayer under his arm. The Kirks both spoke warmly of Bob. They saw him frequently at the church but were unaware of his hoarding. This was not surprising to me, since hoarding disorder is often a hidden secret locked behind closed doors. What had impressed them most was Bob's artistic skills, and coincidentally many of those who suffer from hoarding disorder are quite creative. They remembered his crafted palm crosses for Easter, his handmade Christmas ornaments. They saw him less frequently, they told us, during the last year of his life. I thought about Bob retreating ever more deeply into his self-made fortress.

Our group of six slowly walked to the gravesite that would be Bob's final resting place, with his family. The shared granite headstone for Mike and Marie was engraved with a Russian Orthodox Cross above the name STUKANE. Below that family name were two side-by-side, smoothly polished rectangles, equal in size. These were the places where names and dates could be carved for those buried in the family plot. Within the lower right rectangle, the engraving read: Marie H. Feb. 6, 1997. Normally, the years of a person's birth and death—a lifespan—is noted on a headstone. I thought it odd that for Marie, only the date of her death was carved in stone. No birthdate was included. Making this limited engraving for Marie would have been Mike's decision, as he was alive when Marie died. I had sensed a lack of love between them, noticed no sign of warmth when sorting through their possessions. Valentine's Day, Birthday, Anniversary greeting cards were signed without a mention of "Love." Mike's stark choice raised my suspicions, as did his token remembrance of Marie on her headstone. He did the least he could for her as a husband.

The lower left rectangle, the place for Mike's name and dates of his life and death, was blank. Mike had died in 2005 and he was definitely buried in the spot I was standing on, but his presence was not recognized. Bob, I guess, never got around to having his father's name engraved, nor his life's dates noted. Nothing but a small Masonic logo, the square and compass, was etched into the stone, a carving Mike had likely commissioned long ago. I stared at the empty space and wondered whether Bob's grief was so great that it became an obstacle to any sort of engraving. Anyone looking at the headstone would think only one person, Marie, had been buried in the plot. It was as if Mike were still alive. On the other hand, I now understood that hoarding disorder turns decision-making into an intolerable task. Bob would have needed to hire an engraver and approve words and dates. I could imagine him postponing any final decisions. The headstone would be something he would do on another day, or perhaps the day after, or the day after that.

I was brought back to the moment by the sound of Father Kirk speaking a prayer at the gravesite: "O God, whose blessed Son was laid in a sepulcher in the garden: Bless, we pray, this grave, and grant that he who is to be buried here may dwell with Christ in paradise, and may come to your heavenly kingdom; through your Son Jesus Christ our Lord. Amen." Six of us encircled the square opening in the earth that had been created for Bob's remains. I considered his suffering. He was one of millions of people who lived among hoarded possessions, their stand-ins for comfort and love. A hidden epidemic exists in our midst.

Walking back into St. Mary's Russian Orthodox Church after leaving the gravesite, the same religious icons that I had seen elaborately framed in the Cherry Hill house greeted me. The interior glistened in gold. On golden ten-foot-high poles, surrounded by gold filigree, was the Russian Orthodox image of the Virgin Mary on the left side of an elaborate altar of iconic saints, and to the right was the image of Jesus Christ, identical to icons that watched over me during my year of careful decisions. At a square memorial side altar overseen by a shiny bronze Russian Orthodox crucifix, I lit taper candles in memory of all four of my relatives—Mike, Marie, and Bob, who were buried close by, and for Peter, whose ashes were laid to rest in the small cemetery of Philadelphia's Old Pine Street Church, where he had been musical director.

My next visit to St. Vladimir's Cemetery would be a year later in 2019, to see etched on the original granite headstone's once-vacant rectangular space: Michael M., 1917–2005, and on the ground below, a flat granite grave marker with the words: Son, Robert J. Stukane, 1949–2016. Ellen and I had laid everyone and everything to rest. I had been unprepared for the emotional pull, my strong sense of connection to my extended family, my sadness over the way my cousin Bob had died in his house of hoarding. My year of discovery heightened my awareness of the sustaining power of family ties, no matter how stretched those ties may be. Another revelation was the power of objects to hold the aspirations of their owners. Through their objects, I absorbed the spirit of each family member. The way Bob existed among his piled collections and mountainous debris allowed me to develop a compassionate understanding of hoarding disorder, a condition I had mostly known as the commercialized basis of a television series. It is so much more. My year away from normal routines and into an environment that is separate from me but still attached to me changed my perspective. I wonder now more than I ever have, "What goes on behind closed doors?"

Resources

Links to organizations that offer help for those suffering hoarding disorder, and support for their families, are listed below:

The International OCD Foundation/Hoarding: https://hoarding.iocdf.org/
The IOCDF offers excellent information about hoarding disorder, as well as guidance for finding help.
The International OCD Foundation's "Hoarding Disorder and Buried in Treasures Support Group" on Facebook: https://www.facebook.com/groups/2173610616110515
The Organizer Coach (requires a registration fee) offers a virtual Buried in Treasures sixteen-week workshop: https://theorganizercoach.com/buried-in-treasures
Clutter Image Rating (CIR), a free app created by Boston University offers visual views of what happens inside a home when objects keep accumulating: https://apps.apple.com/us/app/clutter-image-rating/id981642952
The National Association for Productivity and Organizing Professionals (NAPO) can provide direction through counseling: https://www.napo.net/page/howtohire
The Family-As-Motivators Program: explained in an online slide show from Gregory S. Chasson Ph.D., psychologist, associate professor, and director, Behavioral Interventions of the Obsessive-Compulsive and Related Disorders Clinic, University of Chicago: https://www.slideshare.net/slideshow/gregory-chasson-family-support-and-intervention-for-hoarding/64484643
Clutterers Anonymous offers a 12-step recovery program for those who have more possessions than they can handle: https://clutterersanonymous.org/
Academy of Cognitive and Behavioral Therapies can help someone with hoarding disorder find a Cognitive Behavioral Therapist: https://www.academyofcbt.org/

Bibliography

Books

Colwell, Chip. *So Much Stuff: How Humans Discovered Tools, Invented Meaning, and Made More of Everything*. Chicago: University of Chicago Press, 2024.
Falkoff, Rebecca R. *Possessed: A Cultural History of Hoarding*. New York: Cornell University Press, 2021.
Frost, Randy O., and Gail Steketee. *Stuff: Compulsive Hoarding and the Meaning of Things*. New York: Mariner Books, 2011.
Hurd, Barbara. *Entering the Stone: On Caves and Feeling Through the Dark*. Boston, MA: Houghton Mifflin Harcourt, 2008.
Kalman, Maira. *Women Holding Things*. New York: Harper, 2022.
Lidz, Franz. *Ghosty Men*. New York: Bloomsbury, 2002.
McKinley ISTCC, Dr. Mark B. *The Psychology of Collecting: Everybody Collects Something, YES You Do!* Bakersfield, CA: International Society of Talking Clock Collectors, 2015.
Mueller, M. D., Shirley M. *Inside the Head of a Collector: Neuropsychological Forces at Play*. Seattle, WA: Lucia Marquand, 2019.
Slepian, Michael. *The Secret Life of Secrets: How Our Inner Worlds Shape Well-Being, Relationships and Who We Are*. New York: Crown Publishers, 2022.
Steketee, Gail and Christiana Bratiotis. *Hoarding: What Everyone Needs To Know*. New York: Oxford University Press, 2020.
Tolin, David F., Randy O. Frost, and Gail Steketee. *Buried in Treasures: Help for Compulsive Acquiring, Saving, and Hoarding*. New York: Oxford University Press, 2014.
Tompkins, Ph.D., Michael A., and Tamara L. Hartl, Ph.D. *Digging Out: Helping Your Loved One Manage Clutter, Hoarding & Compulsive Acquiring*. Oakland, CA: New Harbinger, 2009.
Trentmann, Frank. *Empire of Things: How We Became a World of Consumers, from the Fifteenth Century to the Twenty-First*. New York: Harper, 2016.
Watson, Lyall. *The Nature of Things: The Secret Life of Inanimate Objects*. Rochester, VT: Destiny Books, 1992.

Zasio, Dr. Robin. *The Hoarder in You: How to Live a Happier, Healthier, Uncluttered Life.* Emmaus, PA: Rodale Books, 2012.

Studies

Chasson, Gregory S., Arryn A. Guy, Sage Bates, and Patrick W. Corrigan. "They Aren't Like Me, They Are Bad and They Are to Blame: A Theoretically-Informed Study of Stigma of Hoarding Disorder and Obsessive-Compulsive Disorder." *Journal of Obsessive-Compulsive and Related Disorders* 16 (2018): 56–65. https://www.sciencedirect.com/science/article/abs/pii/S2211364917301872?via%3Dihub.

Chasson, Gregory S., Ashley Carpenter, Jenna Ewing, Brittany Gibby, and Nancy Lee. "Empowering Families to Help a Loved One with Hoarding Disorder: Pilot Study of Family-as-Motivators Training." *Behaviour Research and Therapy* 63 (2014): 9–16. https://www.sciencedirect.com/science/article/abs/pii/S0005796714001454?via%3Dihub.

Frost, Randy O., and Rachel C. Gross. "The Hoarding of Possessions." *Behaviour Research and Therapy* 31, no, 4 (1993): 367–81. https://www.sciencedirect.com/science/article/abs/pii/000579679390094B?via%3Dihub.

Frost, Randy O., and Tamara L. Hartl. "A Cognitive-Behavioral Model of Compulsive Hoarding." *Behaviour Research and Therapy* 34, no. 4 (1996): 341–50. https://www.sciencedirect.com/science/article/abs/pii/0005796795000712?via%3Dihub.

Tolin, David F., Randy O. Frost, Gail Steketee, and Jordana Muroff. "Cognitive Behavioral Therapy For Hoarding Disorder: A Meta-Analysis." *FOCUS* 19, no. 4 (2021). https://psychiatryonline.org/doi/full/10.1176/appi.focus.19403.

Tolin, David F., Randy O. Frost, Gail Steketee, and Kristin E. Fitcha. "Family Burden of Compulsive Hoarding: Results of an Internet Survey." *Behaviour Research and Therapy* 46, no. 3 (2008): 334–44. https://www.ncbi.nlm.nih.gov/pmc/articles/PMC3018822/.

Van Noppen, Barbara, and Gail Skeketee. "Family Responses and Multifamily Behavioral Treatment for Obsessive-Compulsive Disorder." *Brief Treatment and Crisis Intervention* 3, no. 2 (2003): 231–48. https://www.researchgate.net/publication/247903576_Family_Responses_and_Multifamily_Behavioral_Treatment_for_Obsessive-Compulsive_Disorder.

Newspapers

Ahmir Questlove Thompson, "Questlove: Collecting Is An Act of Devotion, and Creation." *New York Times*, Mary 25, 2022. https://www.nytimes.com/2022/03/25/opinion/questlove-inspiration-collection.html.

Corey Kilgannon, "His Siblings Gathered to Sell the Family Home. Then He Started Shooting." *New York Times*, August 27, 2024. https://www.nytimes.com/2024/08/27/nyregion/murder-suicide-long-island-syosset.html?searchResultPosition=2.

Maravilla, Rafael. "Hoarding Disorders Have Increased in The Pandemic. Here's How to Help a Loved One Who Hoards." *Washington Post*, March 7, 2022. https://www.washingtonpost.com/wellness/2022/03/07/how-to-understand-help-hoarder/.

Article

Jeannette Cooperman. "What's Causing the Rise of Hoarding Disorder?" *JSTOR Daily*, January 16, 2019. https://daily.jstor.org/whats-causing-the-rise-of-hoarding-disorder/.

Family Tree

A Three - Generation Family Tree

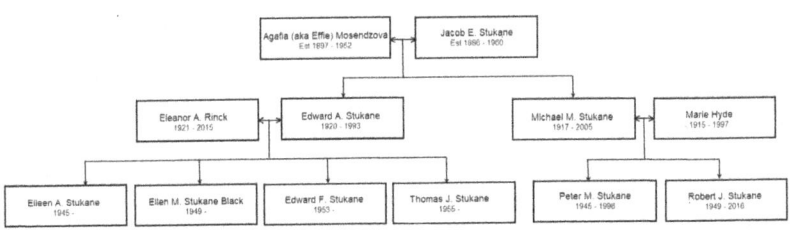

About the Author

Eileen Stukane is the author of *Running on Two Different Tracks*, an ebook memoir of family loss and gain; *The Dream Worlds of Pregnancy*, the psychological journey of mothers-and-fathers-to-be through the trimesters; and she is coauthor of four well-known women's health books, among them *Listen To Your Body* and *The Complete Book of Breast Care*. Eileen became interested in women's health and cultural shifts in society while on the editorial staffs of *Good Housekeeping*, *Cosmopolitan*, and *Self* magazines. As a New York City writer, her articles on those topics have appeared in *Cosmopolitan*, *Harper's Bazaar*, *Glamour*, *McCall's*, *Family Circle*, *Redbook*, *Ladies' Home Journal*, *The Daily News*, *The Huffington Post*, and numerous other national publications. *The House That Held Everything* was born when Eileen confronted rooms densely packed with diverse, hoarded belongings in a family home that she and her siblings had inherited. Her curiosity about what had happened to create such chaos ultimately led to her exploration of hoarding disorder. Across the country, millions of people who accumulate and hoard, are significantly reshaping family relations. Eileen lives in Manhattan with her husband, David Puchkoff. In 2022, she shared a First Place Award from the New York Press Association for her coverage of the arts in ChelseaCommunityNews. For more information about the author, visit her website: www.eileenstukane.com.